Winning
Your
Inner
Battle

Jeanne Heiberg

RESOURCE PUBLICATIONS, INC.
San Jose, California

Editorial director: Kenneth Guentert
Production editor: Elizabeth J. Asborno
Art director: Terri Ysseldyke-All
Production assistant: Eileen Silva

Reprint Department
Resource Publications, Inc.
160 E. Virginia Street, #290
San Jose, CA 95112-5848

Library of Congress Cataloging in Publication Data
available.

5 4 3 2 1 | 93 92 91 90 89

To my dear friends and encouragers,
Tess and Chub Klein.

Contents

Acknowledgments

Thanks to those who encouraged me, who read the manuscript and gave feedback, and who provided friendship and moral support during the work on this book:

Bob Armbruster; Carolyn Blake; Aristide Bruni; Alicia Cavanaugh; John and Marlene Cuniberti; Vern Dethmers; Dorothy Garofalo; Frank Haronian; Bill Hatton; Eric, Kim, and Milton Heiberg; Sue Kirchick; Tess and Chub Klein; Alice Kraemer; Nusia and Yvon LaRoche; Peg Linnihan; Lois MacIntyre; Robert Murphy; Jeanne Nametz; Theodore Osbahr; Steve Peters; Trina Paulus; David and Aurora Protano; Louis Savary; Francis Seymour; Stephen Sheridan; Laurie Stevenson; Helenmarie Sunkenberg; Eugene Tozzi; Patricia Vaillancourt; and Annemarie Williams.

Thanks also to the Belleville Public Library and its wonderful, helpful librarians—Frederick Lewis, Caroline Stahl, and Barbara Dombrowski—who obtained even the most esoteric, out-of-the-way books as needed.

Introduction

A correspondence exists between problems you have to deal with in external life and problems you need to deal with internally, within yourself. You have battles to win in both places.

This book takes a deep look at inner battles. They are more mysterious, less understood, easier to overlook. They are, however, crucial not only to inner health and wholeness but to external success as well.

Inner journeys to inner overcoming put you in touch with resources that help you in external overcoming: problem-solving, fulfillment, and happy living. Powerful insights and energies are available to those who take the time and effort to find them.

In modern America, the temptation is to live life on the surface, a surface that has become quite cluttered. Modern knowledge has changed life enormously. People are more comfortable; they have more material goods and commodities to ease their way through life. But people themselves may sometimes be in danger of becoming a commodity.

As an associate professor of art education at Trenton State College, I often had time on my hands as students worked out creative assignments in class. During one such time, I browsed through a student's sociology textbook, in a section on love and marriage.

The authors "pooh-pooh" any romantic notions; they say marriage and sex are simply marketplace realities. Each contender enters the arena advertising his or her assets to vie for the best deal they can get in a partner. The authors depict one of the most important human relations as a commodity exchange.

This concept limits appreciation of love, sex, the person, and what it means to be human. I was troubled by the authors' insistence on these ideas, and by the full authority of university professors who stood behind them.

Originally, universities intended to help people discover more about the whole universe and the many dimensions of what it means to be human. The great inner universe of a person was missing from the lines I read. That inner universe is the topic this book is primarily concerned with.

Of course, the inner universe of each person is not formed apart from the outer universe, including other people. Environment and the people in it contribute to each person's formation. However, all life, all growth, all choices, all actions begin within. Think of babies hidden in mothers and seeds hidden in flowers or in the earth. Ideas begin in the poet's, artist's, or inventor's head before they take external shape.

Albert Einstein conceived his theory of relativity from within in the middle of the night. It came in a flash, in a vision. Only later did he work out the theories and mathematical formulae. It is significant that the original conception of the idea happened in the darkness of night. The vision, prompted by his conscious work, broke forth in inspired wholeness from his deep self, his creative unconscious: the dark, hidden, and mysterious element present in every human.

The theories that stemmed from Einstein's midnight vision proved valid. They are rapidly changing the earth and space around it. Humans have flown to the moon, launched satellites, and communicated all over the world. Corporations store vast systems of information, and countries hold powerful energies capable of destroying the earth.

Because of the insight that emerged from Einstein's inner mind, everyday life will never be quite the same. What happens inside people inevitably affects what happens outside, in the world they share with others.

Einstein's discoveries also changed the way people think. People now know the universe is not static, rigidly fixed, or motionless. Rather it is constantly in motion and in process, on a great journey. Scientists say it is rapidly expanding.

The human race is also on a journey, developing through many stages, expanding in awareness. Each individual is called to a journey through life that includes many choices, problems, conflicts, and battles. Making the best choices, solving problems, and winning battles will result when people make unseen, inner journey to hidden sources of life.

For those who respond to the call and persevere, the inner journey will result in new information, wisdom, transformation, and final fulfillment. They will touch stores of energies that can either destroy or heal and give life. These people will learn to steer these powers away from destruction toward creativity and life.

Because of the power of inner energies, inner journeys involve territory that sometimes scares people. Those mysterious areas of the human mind—conscious, unconscious, the Self—hold powerful, potential danger and opportunity. The book examines some maps and plans gleaned from previous explorers to help the course of inner journeys and inner overcoming. In this exploration of the human psyche, I consulted psychologists, scientists, mythmakers, storytellers, theologians, scholars, heroes, heroines, and ordinary people. I recommend some external guides—friends, advisors, counselors, spiritual directors—to accompany you in your explorations.

In this book, the words "psyche" and "psychic" simply refer to your inner world. They originate from the Greek word for soul, or spirit, breath, life, and have come to mean "the inner mind." I do not mean "ESP" or "psychic powers" when I use these terms. "Psyche" signifies the unseen, internal world of a human being.

This book also deal with the unconscious mind, which people often find difficult to deal with. It hides barely perceived dangers, yet emits positive power and energy. It has its own laws and reasons, its own honesty and integrity, and its own wisdom. It provides strength. When you win a battle in this inner arena, you win in other, external arenas as well.

Because internal and external worlds are so related, I weave back and forth between the two. Interaction in the outer world contributes to the formation of the inner person or psyche. Such interaction includes experiences with others and choices you make. To focus firmly back on the external, active side of life, the last chapter poses questions of choice, and Appendix 2 offers some choices for life.

In addition to theory, anecdotes and factual information, this book offers imagery meditations to help you with your inner journeys and battles. I hope this book inspires you to win and overcome as your life progresses, and that you have many victory stories to tell along the way.

THE MEDITATIONS

Images are Memorable

A cassette tape I acquired by mistake brought home to me again the mighty power of mental images. It began at the Belleville, N.J. library, where a cassette called *How to Motivate* caught my eye. "Great," I thought. "I work with volunteer teachers, with parents, with students. Plenty of motivation needed; I can use a brushup."

Naturally, when I slipped the tape into my car cassette player, I was anticipating fresh ideas on motivation, but it was the wrong tape. What I got was *How to Improve Your Memory*. I shrugged my shoulders and said, "Oh well, my memory needs improving too."

I was on my way to give a banner-making workshop. In my bag were many visual peace images, along with explanations and motivations, to start people off on a peace quilt. With this in the back of my mind, I heard the cassette speaker reveal the secret of good memory: mental images.

If you want to remember someone's name, you simply form a mental picture to go with each syllable, and you also visualize his face. If it's a phone number you wish to remember, each number must have a symbol to go with it. Energizing the picture with a little action also helps. The heart of the matter is: visual images will help you remember what you would otherwise forget.

I thought of the symbols the families in my workshop would soon be fashioning out of felt and fabric. These images and their meanings would stay with them a long time, forming a deep part of their inner fabric. I thought of the medieval cathedrals with their images in glass and stone. They spoke of deep, basic spiritual realities in ways that people would remember always.

Images Are Transforming

All arts have roots in religions that taught their society basic values. Members of the society learned important ways of relating to their fellow humans, their society, their God. Symbols and stories embodying vivid, unforgettable images allowed ideas and values to seep into the unconscious. There they activated basic archetypes waiting to be drawn into consciousness. This process helped the person in the process of individuation, or transformation into their best possible selves. The power of the symbols lay in energizing of a great waiting potential, a powerhouse waiting to be tapped.

Thus, purely abstract reason lacks the power to deeply transform a person. While abstract reasoning has its own important power and place (I wouldn't want to be without it), by itself it isn't enough. Human healing, wholeness, wisdom, and fullness ask more. The human spirit also needs the help of life-giving, energizing images.

Many psychologists have become aware of the role symbols and images play in enabling people to transcend their limitations and problems. Guided meditations like those presented here are being used in many human development courses. In the summer of 1988, one group alone estimated that over one thousand people across the nation were taking their courses of studies monthly. Medical doctors are making use of imagery to effect both diagnosis and healing. Some religious leaders have also begun to use imagery meditations to help people toward transformation and growth.

The Power of Images

In spiritual circles there has long been a fear of images and imagination because of their power. Bad images can form bad concepts and lead to bad actions. Hollow images can create inner hollowness. A contemporary problem is exemplified on Madison Avenue, where the power of images is well-known. Here are people who pour millions into images for advertising to sell commercial products. Are they concerned with the human spirit or simply with selling?

Rather than abandoning the power of images and arts to the advertisers, why not use them for the real happiness of people? Those concerned with the human and spiritual potential of people will offer something wonderful when they harness the power of images for the highest and greatest growth.

The major religions have always done this, but fresh approaches are needed. Today, many external forces work against inner discovery and growth. The communications media have become so powerful and pervasive that counteraction is necessary. It is more important than ever that people find their own inner center, their wisdom, their powerful places of healing, growth, and transformation.

The images in the meditations are not the only way to do this, but they provide a great and powerful tool.

Introduction

I recommend taking these meditations one by one rather than all at once. You may find using the relaxation techniques in the Appendix helpful. Enter into each one, experience the images, and give them time to speak to you fully. Reflect on what you discover. Experience a little more of life, then return to another meditation.

Use these meditations freely, creatively, altering them and applying them to your own situation, people, and needs. May they be a blessing to you, to your greatest hopes, and to your highest dreams for the human spirit.

1. *Winning Through Inner Journeys to Life*

A PERSONAL JOURNEY

On a hot July night many summers ago, I wandered down a dark path, pillow tucked under my arm, a blanket and sheets draped over my shoulders, looking for a place to sleep. I heard cows breathing heavily as I passed the barn, heading toward what I hoped would be quiet. This was an insomnious period of my life, where the joys of an idealistic community were sometimes dampened by the noise of other idealists. The quiet of a community college on an Ohio farm was even more affected by the influx of many young people for a popular workshop. Their chattering was darling by day, but after eleven the charm for me decreased considerably. The little farmhouses that housed us creaked at each footstep and echoed conversation and laughter loudly through the night. As one of the responsible leaders, I stood in dire need of some heavy zzzs. When, after several nights, I saw no further hope of sleep in my assigned room, I simply rose, gathered up the necessaries, and journeyed hopefully down the road. After trying many creative possibilities including a barn and a corn crib, I managed to survive and function.

TO LIVE IS TO CHANGE

The workshop ended with a festive closing dinner, at which all were given a message tied to a flower. Mine read, "To live is to change, and to be perfect is to change often," words of John Henry Cardinal Newman. Though I received it by chance, the message seemed appropriate. The student who wrote the text told me that mine was included at the insistence of the school's director, who came by while she was at her task. We both decided it was destined for me, to help me see the bright side of my forced changes.

This message helped me see the bright side of many later changes, and my life has been full of them. I've moved to different parts of the country, changed jobs and homes, made new friends, found new relationships, solved new sets of problems, and counted on new kinds of securities. All this has been stressful in varying degrees. Through all of it, I believe I have grown and expanded. I haven't achieved Newman's perfection by a long shot; I feel a long way from that. However, I'm still in process, on the journey, and I look forward to further possibilities.

THE INNER JOURNEY

One of the greatest areas of growth so far has been to see the degree to which a person's own attitudes and choices affect happiness. You carry inside yourself wonderful hidden resources waiting, like buried treasures, to be discovered and liberated. The greatest, most fundamental journey is within, to where you touch and tap this treasure. Here you find sources of Life that bring the greatest growth to fulfillment.

Inner journeys are not the easiest to make. En route there are dragons and dangers to overcome. The fairy and folk tales of old give a good psychic picture. In his book *The Hero with a Thousand Faces*, the great myth and symbol scholar Joseph Campbell offers a rich

anthropological resource of stories of heroes.[1] Their
heroic journeys led them into dangers and difficulties,
but in overcoming these they obtained a great prize.

EXTERNAL AND INTERNAL BATTLES

On the journey of life, you are sure to meet external
difficulties and sometimes dangers. Life is full of them.
They are often, however, reflections of inner difficulties
and dangers, conflicts, and crises of the psyche. The
external noise that made it hard for me to get my zzzs,
and the work obligations I wanted to fulfill certainly
posed problems. I did have to work at a more workable
situation. However, the greatest problem was my own
reaction to exuberant, less-than-thoughtful young
people, inadequate living arrangements, and taxing work
challenges with less than professional provisions. At the
time I thought *they* were the monsters. Later I discovered
bigger monsters inside. The real battleground was in my
own thoughts, feelings, and attitudes. Only by dealing
with these could more growth and expanded life be
possible. I also discovered that handling the inner battles
led to more creative and successful handling of external
problems as well.

With good choices, the obstacles, conflicts, and crises
actually become the source of your greatest growth and
expansion. It all depends on what stance you take, what
direction you decide on. If you make the primary journey
into your own inner world, you will certainly meet
problems, conflicts and dangers also on this deeper level.
Ultimately, however, like the heroes and heroines of
folklore, you will also win a great and precious prize.

THE QUEST OF THE HERO
AND HEROINE

Let's take a look at heroes and heroines to find a basic
pattern. The usual tale is often about an apparently
external adventure. The typical hero of many myths,

stories, and legends is first found in his home by the familiar hearth, or in the village, the ordinary, everyday place where he grew up. Most of his peers will live their whole lives in this place. However, some crisis or need will start our hero on a journey or quest. There is some great problem to be solved, some great good to be achieved.

As the hero sets out on his journey, he often meets others, people or animals, often with urgent needs. By listening and helping, by giving kindness and respect even to those who are helpless, old, or ugly, the hero acquires friends. The new friends give guidance, advice, magic words, or weapons that will later prove helpful when our hero meets dangers on the way. A great good isn't easily achieved. Witches, evil sorcerers, monsters, dreadful dragons and all kinds of uglies bar the way. However, with courage and pure intention, with wisdom and weapons from friends, our hero will prevail; victory will eventually be his. He will achieve the great good; he will win the prize.

Of course, the traveler may sometimes be a she, a heroine. Think of that famous American seeker, Dorothy, on the yellow brick road to Oz. She has to overcome the evil witch before achieving her heart's desire, a return to her home and loved ones. In her quest, Dorothy finds friends along the way: the scarecrow, the tin man, and the cowardly lion. Because she is kind and helpful, they join her and help her through the dangers of the quest. In an interesting variation, they also have their hearts' desires, their goals to achieve, on the journey: an intelligent mind, a loving heart, and courage—all things of value.

INNER RESOURCES

Two significant factors stand out in the story of Dorothy and her friends. First, Oz is a mythical world, symbolic of Dorothy's inner life. The friends she meets there, however, resemble people in her "real," Kansas life. The scarecrow, the tin man, and the lion of Oz are symbols of inner resources to help her on an "inner journey." But their images derive from real-life friends. Both external and internal friends are needed on the journey, and frequently they overlap, with one as an image of the other.

The second significant factor relates to the prizes sought by heroes and heroines. The good things the Oz friends seek through so many adventures are, at the end, already available to them, within themselves. The scarecrow is actually smart, the tin man loving, the lion brave, but they have to discover these qualities for themselves. Dorothy, too, is able to "go home" whenever she wishes.

You also have the capacity to "go home" to your deepest source of being, which is already present within yourself. Like Dorothy and her friends, however, you have to make a journey to bring these prizes to your conscious mind. It is only then that you reap the benefit for yourself and others.

PSYCHIC PRIZES:
THE ENRICHED RETURN

The people of Oz and many other stories show that people who quest do not set out on journeys for small reasons. In older tales, a hero seeks the sacred fire, the healing herb, the waters of life, or the Holy Grail. Sometimes the prize will be a beautiful princess, rescued from captivity or death. This prize, this great good, is always a symbol of life. Your typical princess promises love, babies, family, happiness. Your magic herb or sacred flame is the means to eternal life and happiness. The Holy Grail represents a wasteland restored to peace and prosperity, with happiness for all the inhabitants.

In his book *The Hero With a Thousand Faces*, Joseph Campbell suggests that the hero's outer journey symbolizes an inner journey into the psyche. The friends spring from an inner wisdom, the monsters from inner dangers. The journey carries the seeker to that inner place of encounter with the source of all life, the great "I Am." Meetings with God and the creative Holy Spirit take place in quiet, in the deep recesses of the heart.

After overcoming and achieving the prize, heroes and heroines return to their villages, to Kansas, to ordinary consciousness, to the surface of life, bearing the prize: The princess, the gift, the wisdom, the loving heart, the courage, the boon, the life sign. They are enriched and thus able to bring riches to others. So the person who journeys within and encounters the great "I Am," returns enriched—more able to be in touch with all else that is, more able to encounter God and the sources of life in ordinary people, in ordinary situations. Now they are more able to bring healing and life to others.

MORE TALES OF THE JOURNEY

Campbell's "inner journey" interpretation of tales is supported by the earliest recorded story we have. It comes from the ancient Sumerians of the middle-Eastern fertile crescent. The hero is a king named Gilgamesh,[2] who decides to go on a quest to find the herb of Life, a plant with healing powers and the secret of eternal life. This herb is found at the bottom of the seas. Since water is, in literature, symbolic of the unconscious, we have an early mythical clue: the secret of life is found deep within the self. Gilgamesh finds the herb, but a serpent steals it away from him. It is another story in which, like Adam and Eve, evil trickery deprives humans of everlasting life.

Later heroes and heroines were more fortunate. They find and keep the life-giving good. This is especially true of stories in the Bible, as we shall see later. It is also true of the fairy tales I loved as a child. My favorites, as a little girl, involved princes and princesses, and my instinctive fascination and awe were right. He, the prince or knight, is a sign of the human on a vital journey, while she, the princess, is a symbol of wholeness, happiness, increased life. In the Bible and in childhood myths and fairy tales, entropy does not have the last word.

DEFEATING ENTROPY

Entropy, a law of thermodynamics, illustrates Campbell's theory from another dimension. **Entropy** is the measure of disorder of any system. In the external world, entropy is always increasing: things are always running down, disintegrating, wearing out, rusting, rotting, going to pieces, reverting to chaos, and dying. There is a definite downhill principle to the way things are.

Fortunately there is another principle, that of birth, growth, life. You see it in nature as people warmly welcome spring and nurture newborn babies. However there is also an inner dimension to be realized. As a human, you are called to participate in the creation and nurturing of life not only on physical levels but also on deeper, spiritual planes. Wisdom and happiness means doing this to the best of your gifts and abilities. The greatest heroes and heroines are inspiring examples of those who make possible more birth, growth, healing, and renewal of life.

Consider the heroine in the book of Judith.[3] Chaos and entropy engulf Judith's world, as General Holerfernes brings soldiers and war to her land. Her city is under siege; people suffer from hunger and thirst and are ready to surrender. Surrender means exile, slavery, suffering, slaughter, the complete collapse of Judith's people and their world—entropy at its worst.

When the elders of the city decide to surrender to Holerfernes, Judith, a beautiful and deeply religious widow, goes to the elders and asks them to wait. She has a plan.

Before carrying out her external plan, Judith goes on a quiet inner journey of prayer and fasting. Only after this does she dress herself in her best and go out of the city on an external journey to the camp of Holerfernes. After intoxicating the general first with her beauty, then with wine, she slays him and returns to the city with his head as proof of her deed. Her people then route the leaderless invaders and the country returns to peace. While Judith's trophy is not my favorite in the lore of heroes and heroines, it does prove her courage, and it testifies to a victory over entropy and a decisive route of evil.

THE JOURNEY TO LIFE

The Bible and folklore are filled with "Journey to Life" stories: Abraham, Jacob, Joseph, Moses, Paul, and the other apostles. More recent stories and novels also abound with journeys: *Don Quixote, Gulliver's Travels, Robinson Crusoe, Passage to India, Ship of Fools, The Old Man and the Sea.* While these describe outer journeys of varying lengths, most great stories outline inner journeys of overcoming and growth.

One victory story stands out above all others. Joseph Campbell relates all hero and heroine stories to the one of Jesus' death and resurrection. Here is the ultimate hero who makes a journey past even the dragons of crucifixion, death, and descent into dark Hades. But he is also the hero who brings back to humankind the ultimate boon, a new kind of life on a whole new level, a God-life that will outlast all the entropy, death, and destruction there is. Jesus, as the Hero of heroes, finds the secret source of increased and eternal life and gives it to his friends.

Such friends—all those people, in fact—who want to be creative and life-giving, need to enter also into their own inner journey. Every human is called to special ways of overcoming entropy and chaos, according to their gifts. All are invited to create "cosmos," life, and new human possibilities. Your role as a co-creator of Cosmos on many levels—human harmony, healing, and reconciliation—will be explored later.

ENFORCED CHANGES

Often it is the enforced changes, the crosses, the crises of life that bring a person to where he or she can be effective. Sometimes it is only hard things endured that transform an ordinary person into a life-giving presence to others. That is why you have periods of pain, problem, and stress, as well as periods of tranquillity and happiness. That is why life is, in Newman's words, about change, and why you have to "change often" on the way to perfection and wholeness.

When you focus on positive goals and understand possible meaning behind the difficulties, you can tackle problems with greater elan. When you know what the dragons are, you can overcome them. When you know your inner friends and helpers and the weapons at your disposal, you can use them to reach the prize.

NEW NEEDS AND CHALLENGES

Scripture and spiritual traditions have given good guidance for a long time. Great world religions have provided paths for many. However, religious meanings and practices have been abused and bent to self-serving, sometimes evil ends. Even well-meaning people are prone to imprison Spirit in cultural forms originally meant to preserve and pass on what heroes and heroines taught us long ago. The forms become a substitute for the real inner journey, the true encounter with God.

In addition, new dangers and imbalances have come about that hinder inner journeys. Along with many positive contributions, science and technology have made serious inroads on spiritual and human health. A multitude of external wonders, a plethora of things, snowballing mountains of information serve to distract present-day people from the most essential sources of wisdom.

On the other hand, new knowledge has been discovered that, in tandem with solid spiritual roots, will help people to right the imbalances, overcome obstacles and once again claim prizes: wisdom, healing, and wholeness, with increased life both now and in the world to come.

A Meditation for the Journey

PRE-MEDITATION

Put yourself and any others who take this meditation journey in a relaxed state to start. Look over the relaxation exercises in the Appendix to see if any of the techniques will help you or your group. This kind of meditation in itself provides receptive people with a sense of peace and well-being, and you may simply use it as it is.

According to the needs of your group, you may use all of it in a long session, or segments of it, stopping after the first or second encounter. If you end after the first or second encounter, skip to the closing reflections. If the meditation moves on to the third encounter, however, it should continue to the end.

If a group is new to guided meditation (explained more fully in the introduction), you might explain that people have wonderful inner senses, related to their external senses of sight, hearing, smell, taste, and touch. The inner senses, combined with memory and imagination, help you make inner journeys through which you are able to reflect on life, solve problems, and find strength, hope, and healing.

THE MEDITATION

Get into a comfortable position, relax, and take a few deep breaths. Gently close your eyes and sink into a deeper relaxation. Picture yourself walking on a road through green and sunny fields, with farms and houses in the distance. You are headed toward a forest that leads to a mountain. You are on a journey of discovery.

Everything around you is as fresh and natural as the daisies that grow along the edge of the road. You are leaving cities and towns to search for one of the secrets of life you will find at the top of the mountain.

The First Encounter

You draw closer to the forest and see how shady it is compared to the sunny fields you leave behind. As you enter the forest, the path becomes harder to see as it winds through ferns, bushes, and shadows. You stop to get your bearings. Then, in the shadows, you notice an old woman with a wise and kindly face. She smiles at you in a friendly way and asks you where you want to go. You tell her some of your hopes and goals.

The woman nods and smiles as you speak and promises to help you. But first, she asks you for a gift. It is something life asks of you right now. What is it? It is summed up in a symbol or word that you give to the old woman.

The kindly old woman is pleased with your gift and she gives you one in return, wrapped up in a white box and tied with a golden ribbon. This gift will help you on your journey. You eagerly open the box and look within to find your gift: a symbol or word that rests on a golden pillow. What is the gift? Can you tell, at this point, how it will help you?

Now the old woman reassures you that you can always call on her, and on the gift she has given you, for help. She will be waiting for you in this quiet forest whenever you want to return.

The Second Encounter

The old woman points out the path to take and tells you that you will soon meet another friend. You thank her and set out on the path.

You journey deeper into the forest with greater confidence. The shadows are also deeper now, but sun still trickles through the trees in golden patterns, and you hear the fresh murmur of a stream nearby. Your path leads down toward where the stream meanders through lush green ferns and moss-covered rocks. You reach it and sit down on a large rock to rest. Then you notice a kindly, wise old man sitting on another rock nearby.

The old man smiles and waves; he asks you about your journey and you tell him where you are at this point.

The old man nods in encouragement and promises to help you. But first, he asks you for a gift. He wants a symbol or word that spells out a difficulty, a problem you face, something that needs overcoming at this stage of your life's journey. What is this gift you will give him?

You give the old man your gift. He accepts. He tells you that your journey is good, but there is a dragon, a beast, along the way that you will need to overcome. What is this dragon for you right now? Let him tell you about it.

Now the old man reassures you that you need not be afraid; you have all you need to overcome the dragon and he gives you a gift that will help. He hands it to you on a golden pillow. What is this gift that will help you overcome the dragon? Take it gratefully, whether or not you understand its meaning. Thank the old man.

The old man may have more to say about this gift and how it will help you, or give further advice about this stage of your journey and those to come. Listen a while.

The Third Encounter

It's time to move on. Thank the old man, get up, and continue on the forest path that you can see more clearly now. It begins to ascend as it leads up toward the mountain that is your destination. The trees grow further apart here and there is more light as the path breaks through the forest.

Suddenly, as you step out into a clearing, you see a huge red dragon and hear its roar. The dragon stands between you and the path you wish to follow. This dragon speaks of something in your life that needs overcoming right now.

In order to go forward you must overcome this dragon. You take out the gifts that were given to you by your forest friends and hold them out as you walk forward. The dragon begins to shrink, begins to grow smaller and smaller. Now it is afraid of you; it wants to run away, but you seize it and ask it for a gift. The dragon gives you a gift: a wooden treasure chest. You thank the dragon; then, because it's harmless now, you chase it away. Open the chest to find what treasures it contains for you.

Again, it is time to move on. Place all your gifts and treasures in a knapsack and begin to climb the mountain. The path rises sharply. It is hard work, but you want to discover one of the secrets of life so you keep going until you reach the top. From the mountaintop you can see a great distance. You have a wider, broader view of your life than you had before. You can see better where your life is going and what you want to do.

Now, at the top of the mountain, you will receive one of the secrets of life. Sit down, ready yourself, and listen to hear what it is. Be quiet and open as this special gift, the best of all, is given to you.

Closing Reflections

Reflect a little further on the gifts that have been given to you on this inner journey. What do they mean? How will they help you?

Prepare yourself to return from this inner journey renewed, refreshed, feeling wonderful, and ready to live your life with energy and love.

When you have finished your journey, quietly open your eyes.

POST-MEDITATION

Draw a picture of your journey on large sheets of newsprint. Circle the high points. Reflect on the images, symbols, gifts, and words you received. If possible, discuss these with supportive people. Use the bibliography as sources for further work. Do research on the symbols you received to expand and deepen your understanding.

2. *Journey Past Fear*

DEALING WITH FEAR

Fear is one of the biggest obstacles on any journey. This dragon lies in the way of almost all great goals. Tobit, a Hebrew Bible journey tale, provides valuable information on how to deal with this dragon.[1]

The telling part of this story involves a fish, an appropriate symbol for an inner journey. Delving into your inner world surfaces all kinds of interesting things; it's like fishing in deep waters. Indeed, the ocean is a symbol of the unconscious, teeming with unseen life, full of dangers and possibilities.

AN ANCIENT FISH STORY

In this fish story, Tobit's son, Tobiah, goes on a journey with a guide to show him the route. This guide is none other than the angel Raphael, disguised as a fellow Hebrew in exile. He guides Tobiah on the journey from Ninevah to Media to bring back a sum of money deposited by his father, Tobit. Tobit is a good man who often helped his fellow Jews in exile, but now his own fortunes have fallen. Not only does he need money, but he also has been accidentally blinded.

On the journey, a danger threatens. Tobiah goes into the waters of the Tigris river to bathe, only to be attacked by a large fish. Raphael tells him to seize the fish, urging Tobiah not to let it get away. After the fish is landed, the guide instructs the young man to remove and keep the gall, heart, and liver for future use. Later, these organs prove valuable to Tobiah in achieving important goals. The bulk of the fish provides food for the journey; the heart and liver are burnt on the incense embers much later when Tobiah marries Sarah, daughter of the man who holds the money Tobiah is to collect.

Sarah's previous seven husbands had all died on their wedding nights, before the marriages could be consummated. This was the work of a jealous demon and also, perhaps, of fate, because Sarah is meant for Tobiah. Luckily, the demon can't tolerate the burning fish organs, or the prayers, or the patience Tobiah brings with him to the bridal chamber. After three nights of fish incense and Tobiah's abstinence and prayer, the demon leaves forever and Sarah becomes the rightful and happy wife of Tobiah.

There is more. When Tobiah and his bride return to Ninevah, he uses the fish gall as medicine to cure the blindness of his father. The big fish that had attacked Tobiah at the start of the journey becomes the means by which the problems are solved and dreams realized. The big fish helps overcome evil, heals, nourishes, secures love, and increases life for the hero.

This charming biblical novelette with a happy ending has, like all good myths and legends, much to teach about psychic life. Tobiah's journey might symbolize an external journey of life, or an inner one. The fish story, however, alerts us to an inner happening, since it threatens and is overcome in the waters of the Tigris. Since water is a symbol of unconscious life, the fish symbolizes a threat from Tobiah's own inner, unconscious world.

SURFACING THE THREAT

When you are faced with a threat, an inner danger, running away from it is not the best thing to do. It is better to seize it and bring it up into your conscious life where it can be explored. Here Raphael is a good spiritual guide, the model of a good counselor, spiritual advisor, or confessor. Knowledge of what is going on inside can protect you from your own inner demons, those negative, dark, hard-to-face sides of yourself that are a part of your human makeup. The demon that demolishes Sarah's previous husbands waits in Tobiah's future, but he is also waiting inside Tobiah. Tobiah's courage in facing and surfacing a previous threat, along with patience and prayer, saves him and allows him to claim Sarah, the life-giving, love-bestowing prize. Facing rather than fleeing the fish enables the hero to realize his dream, claim his destiny, and bring healing to at least two loved ones: his wife and his father.

Tobiah provides a good model for your own personal pilgrimage. You too need a good guide, such as Raphael, who will help you surface your own inner threats. You will also realize your own destiny, claim your own life prizes, and develop gifts for others when you face rather than flee your own inner world, even when it appears threatening.

THE CURE IN THE DANGER

In Tobiah's story, the threatening danger turns out to be the cure. Whenever a danger or crisis seems to be surfacing in your life, you may be sure that, in the long run, there is something good for you there, something that will bring healing, growth, and wisdom. Some part of the very threat also holds your good. This is a paradox sometimes seen in modern medicine. Vaccination isn't pleasant—I avoid it when I can. But a small, safe portion of the very disease that could harm me has also protected me from some awful ills.

Homeopathy,[2] developed by C. F. S. Hahnemann, is a method by which the medicinal cure, taken in highly diluted, small doses, mimics the disease. People are cured by a controlled portion of something similar to the cause of the distress. This is a finely tuned process and should only be practiced by well-trained doctors.

The ancient symbol of medicine, a snake wrapped around a staff, offers further food for reflection. It comes from two different cultures: Greek, where healing centers featured snakes, and Hebrew, where a snake story tells of a cure.

GETTING THE PICTURE

During the Exodus journey, the Hebrews complain too much about their desert hardships.[3] They are punished with a plague of poisonous serpents, and many die of snakebite. After acknowledging that they sinned in their complaints and lack of trust, the people ask Moses to pray for them. Moses is directed to make a bronze serpent, an image of the deadly snakes. All who look at this image recover from their snakebites.

First the people had to become aware of their wrongdoing. Next, they had to have an image, or picture of the danger, and with that they find healing. In many cases of contemporary cures, "getting a picture" of the danger is also a part of the cure. Though evidence of this is just beginning on the physical level (to be further discussed in the next chapter), it is further along in psychic matters. Psychologists say that drawing the contents of the unconscious into our conscious mind leads not only to healing, but also to increased strength and growth, to individuation as a person.

SURFACING THE SUPPRESSED

The Tobiah story is a grand revelation of the psychic world. Inner dangers often arise from a portion of the psyche that has been suppressed and unexpressed. A part of your personality with gifts to give to your total well-being is not allowed into conscious life. That part becomes distorted, ugly. It builds up energy until it pushes its way through the gates of ego-awareness and threatens harm. If you run away from this part of yourself, continue to suppress it, more danger threatens your well-being. This area of energy will get back at you in sneaky, back-handed ways, or it will build up enough power to erupt dangerously.

However, if you find a good spiritual guide, your own Raphael, and grab onto the danger even as it threatens (because that means it is also surfacing), you are able to make use of it. The very danger becomes your good. Some examples of active imagination at work will make this more clear.

THE WAKING DREAM

Active imagination is a way of surfacing wisdom from the unconscious by bringing people to a relaxed state and calling forth images, symbols, and mental pictures. What appears is often also called a "waking dream," because, like the images from our nighttime dreams, they reveal so much about our present needs and future possibilities.

The first issue of *Synthesis* contains the fascinating discoveries of a client, Sharon, as she is guided by her "Raphael," in this case the author of the article, James Vargiu, and his wife.[4] Sharon was experiencing depression and a block barring the use of her considerable creative gifts. She is portrayed as a beautiful, intelligent young woman, highly gifted but unable to often make use of these gifts. She felt barriers preventing a real contribution. At the first interview, she expressed hard-to-define feelings of anxiety, confusion, general hostility, disgust, even despair in her life.

As Sharon's guides used active imagination to explore her inner world, a powerful symbol emerged, that of an old hag, twisted and ugly. This was a threatening image that filled Sharon with a feeling of disgust. However, Sharon was wise enough to recognize this old hag as part of her own personality she could not get rid of. Instead, she began to carry on a dialogue with this inner image.

She discovered that the hag didn't want to be twisted and ugly, instead she wanted to be recognized. The hag eventually revealed herself as the practical side of Sharon's nature that had been suppressed in favor of her idealistic side. The hag represented a part of her that could be strong, vital, with valuable energies to help Sharon realize her idealistic goals. All the poor hag needed was a little recognition and respect, not suppression. Previously, Sharon recognized only her idealistic side and buried all her less-than-perfect qualities—envy, anger, ambition—in her unconscious. Her hag brought all this to light and helped her to see what she was doing.

Further processes helped Sharon integrate her idealistic and practical energies so that her ambitions and idealism found help rather than blockage. This happened only when she caught and brought to the surface the inner threat symbolized by the hag.

One of my good friends, Marie, had a similar experience. She was working hard on her pastoral ministry degree. For a while, all her time went into studies, research, papers, and lectures. She began to feel stress and anxiety, and noticed a large weight gain due to constant snacking. Feelings of distress grew, and Marie knew something was wrong. She decided to put her active imagination to work. During a waking daydream she herself initiated, an Indian appeared, handsome but threatening. He was dressed in full war bonnet and war paint.

Marie knew enough about inner symbolic language to understand that this war chief represented an inner part of herself that was dangerously in need of getting back to the earth, of living a more natural and balanced life. The Indian kept coming back into her waking dreams until she was able to spend more time on simple activities such as gardening, cooking, swimming, and walking, which brought balance back into her life. If she hadn't heeded this message, Marie might have reaped a heap of trouble from her hidden dark side. The inner image, like Tobiah's fish, represented the means to healing, wholeness and happiness.

THE SLEEPING DREAM

While the guided daydream, or active imagination, is a fairly recent tool for exploring the dark side, the sleeping dream has a long history, going back to the bible and other early records.

One Malaysian tribe called the Senoi built much of their culture around the sleeping dream. From early childhood, youngsters were taught to remember and recount their dreams. Breakfast became a family fantasy feast, when inner psyches were explored through the recounting of the previous night's dreams. Kilton Stewart, the anthropologist who made this discovery, reported that the Senoi were also among the world's most peaceful, balanced, happy people, so we might learn something from their dream culture.[5]

If Senoi children dreamt of a threat, such as a big fish or dangerous animal attacking, or a threatening warrior pursuing, they were taught not to run away but to stand and fight the danger, calling on dream friends to help. They were to fight until the enemy was overcome, then ask for a gift from the vanquished foe. The dangerous creature had to give the gift. Even the most threatening dream images became a source of well-being and growth.

The Senoi recognized that dream images represent a part of the self that needs recognition. Your inner energies, represented by the symbols in your dreams, have gifts to give you. No part of you is waste or junk; all that you are can contribute to your good and the good of those around you, if you are of good will and in touch with your inner wisdom. The New Testament St. Paul said that "all things work together for good to those that love the Lord." His "all things" include not only your external experiences but also your inner world.

OVERCOMING INNER AND OUTER FEARS

Sometimes overcoming inner fear dovetails with overcoming fears evoked by outer threats. There is always at least a subtle relationship, but I had an experience that made the relationship quite vivid. Inspired by the Senoi, I faced a venomous, dangerous dream snake that threatened innocent dream children. I overcame the snake and demanded more courage.

Shortly after, in waking life, it fell to my lot to discourage a rather tough-looking motorcycle gang from creating a disturbance in a field near my home. At first I shouted across a wide distance that a baby was sleeping and an old person was sick, and that we all needed quiet. Looking their toughest, they gestured to me to come closer, if I dared. Now I'm not one for taking physical risks—I look anything but formidable—but the thought of the Senoi crossed my mind, along with David and a few others. As I strode forward, the whole gang turned around and zoomed away. I found it interesting that my courage improved right after I overcame a fear in my dreams, and that I could then send a motorcycle gang packing.

COMMUNITIES FACING DANGER

Facing fears, dangers, and even evils has other external and group implications. Just as Tobiah found healing and strength through grasping and surfacing the threatening fish, so groups can also take hold of their dangers. Communities as well as individuals grow through facing rather than burying problems. The value of bringing evils to light has been demonstrated by Amnesty International, the organization that raises money to publicize and protest the imprisonment, torture, and inhumane treatment of innocent, non-violent political prisoners. The thesis of this group is that injustice, cruelty, and evil cannot face the light of public scrutiny. Bringing evils to light is half the battle in their banishment.

The Roman Catholic Church has also been rediscovering this idea in the resurrection of an ancient ritual called "scrutinies" practiced by early Christians. Part of the new RCIA (Rite of Christian Initiation of Adults),[6] scrutinies provide a practical format for communal searching and facing of dangers. They also provide a proper, positive approach.

SCRUTINIZING EVIL

Scrutinies are rituals that take place in certain Sunday Masses during Lent. They are part of the preparation for **catechumens,** adults who are preparing for initiation into the Roman Catholic Church at the important Easter Vigil. The scrutinies have roots going back to the second century, when the newly formed Christian communities faced many dangers and evils as a persecuted minority in a flagrantly immoral culture. The rituals were developed to help initiates deal with the difficulties they would face as Christians.

Many modern adults cringe at the thought of undergoing a scrutiny, believing at first that they will be the object of criticism. Most are relieved to find that these are rituals for healing and strengthening, and that the hindrances to their growth, not themselves, are the objects of exploration.

In some places, catechumens meet with their sponsors and guides to discuss all the things that could possibly hinder them from fully living the Christian life they are preparing for. What could threaten their full healing or block the living out of their baptismal vows? What are their fears? What could lessen love or the giving of their gifts in service to others? What might hinder the growth of God's reign in themselves, in others, in their community, country, and world?

After a list of hindrances is made, they are worked into a litany with a suitable response: "O Lord, deliver us";

"Free us, Lord"; or, "Lord, hear our prayer." The litany is then prayed by the whole community at the appropriate Masses.

When a group does its work well, amazing power can be felt in the exorcisms of all the fears, evils, dangers, and blocks. Facing rather than fleeing is the answer on both personal and group levels.

Scrutinies are done as prayer rituals in the context of a Lenten journey with Jesus up to Jerusalem, through death, to resurrection. The appropriate biblical readings proclaim Christ's power over infirmity and death. A blind man is given sight and dead Lazarus is called forth from the dark of the tomb to life. The scrutinies echo this calling forth for catechumens and faithful. God's people have within them power and strength to confront the dark, dangerous side of the world, with its threats to fullness and life. The scrutinies, the looks at the dangers, are taken in the context of God's power to overcome for them and in them.

Even the most ardent initiates are not meant to look continuously at fears, threats, and dangers. The main focus is on the goal, on God, on the fullness and wholeness of the life they are growing toward. And they are not expected to take their look at the dangers alone. Like Tobiah, they need a guide. Their exploration is carried out with prayer, reflection, and scripture in a communal context, in the company of faith-full companions. The same focus on community, guides, positive goals, and God are recommended balances to your grappling, in your own cultural/spiritual context, with inner and outer needs, fears, and dangers.

Meditation on Fishing

PRE-MEDITATION

The seashore is an ideal place for you to go to be
renewed. It is a place where you can become more
relaxed, more open to your inner wisdom and sources of
healing.

The ocean is awesome—so vast, so powerful, so
teeming with unseen life. All life on earth is said to have
originated in the sea. Each human life also begins
cradled by water. Sages say that, spiritually, humans are
like fish swimming in a sea of God's love. The sea, in this
sense, is an image of God the Creator, the Source of Life.

Poets and novelists have symbolized the sea as the
unconscious mind casting up treasures at unexpected
moments like shells upon the shore or like fishes in a net.

Anne Morrow Lindbergh wrote a classic called *Gifts
from the Sea*. She meditated on shells that became for
her symbols of wisdom from the creative unconscious.
Many other people have meditated on things from the
sea; some of their insights are included in the following
reading.

This prayer and reading will help you relax and be
open to your own gifts of inner wisdom.

Prayer

"Thank you, Creator God, for bringing us to a time
and place of peace and relaxation. Thank you for the

gifts you will give to us. Create in us a quietness, an openness, that we will be prepared to receive your treasures. Amen."

Reading

From *Contemplation and the Art of Saladmaking,* chapter 1, "Small is Beautiful Salad: The Fish." (Optional scripture reading: Matthew 13:48.)

Fish have always been a symbol of abundance, fertility, life, and new life. Consider the hundreds of eggs fish produce and the endless variety and number of fish.

The water fish swim in is a symbol of life. It cradles beginning physical life, and, through baptism, it cradles beginning spiritual life.

The fish, swimming in its natural element, water, seems liberated, free, at home. Hebrews compared fish to the wisdom-seeking, faithful people of Israel swimming in their natural element, the waters of Torah. Through Torah they drew wisdom out of their own inner deep.

Buddhists saw a fish on the footprint of Buddha as a symbol of freedom from restraints, liberation from purely earthly attachments and desires. Buddha,...like the Christ, was a fisher of men and women for freedom.

Small fish, for early Christians, signified followers of the great fish, Christ, in whom they were liberated from sin and death into resurrection and freedom by baptism with water. These little fish were inspired to share what they had with others in order to focus on God's kingdom, where there is true abundance.

But the Kingdom of God is within. That is the place to cast nets and lines to reap bounty. Interestingly, Jesus first chose fishermen as followers, promising to make them fishers of men and women. But to fish for people, you must fish *in* each person, in the deep soul, through prayer, meditation, study, loving thought, and action.

THE MEDITATION

Imagine yourself on the shore of the ocean. You are sitting in the dunes, feeling safe, secure, warmed by the sun. You gaze on the wideness of the water before you, watching the waves travel in rhythm. The swells sparkle in the sun, rise to a rippling froth, and grow more intense as they near the shore.

Your gaze wanders from the near shore across the large expanse of waves and water, past fishing boats and ships, until it meets the horizon, where water meets sky. There mists rise and clouds form so that it is difficult to see where water ends and sky begins.

Underneath this vast expanse is rich, churning life. You see people fishing in their boats, patiently waiting for a bite. Beneath the water are fish of all kinds: blues, mackerels, dolphins, whales, shellfish, clams, crabs, sea horses, seaweed, and other creatures too small to see.

You watch the people fishing, admiring their patience. How do they know when the surprise will come when they will feel the tug and find a fish on their line?

You are here now to become more open and receptive not only to the ocean of external geography but also to the ocean of your own internal geography. Here you have time to look into the distant horizons of your past and future to see how waves of thoughts, ideas, and experiences are breaking on your shores of consciousness. Now you have time to be quiet, to feel the tug of a thought, idea, or inspiration that wants to surface and be part of your conscious reality.

Now picture yourself getting up and walking along the shore until you see shells that want you to look at them. You pick one up, a gift from the sea. What does this shell say to you? What treasure is the ocean of God's love giving you at this moment? Be open to it now.

Thank the Creator for this gift. Ask God to send you more during the coming days: more shells, fish, inner treasures, and gifts of wisdom from that place inside you where the creative power is at work, where the Spirit of God touches your life. Thank God for this richness that exists in you.

Now a fishing boat is coming to the shore. Friendly people motion you aboard. You think of the risk in going right out over the water, but they are skilled boaters and you want to catch some fish. When you reach deeper water, you lower your line and wait. You wonder what new treasure the sea will have for you, what new thought, idea, or inspiration will surface to help you in your life right now.

Suddenly, something tugs your line. Reel in the line to bring up a hidden treasure to your conscious mind. Look and listen as God gives you a special message.

When you are finished fishing, thank God and your inner wisdom. Mentally row back to shore and open your eyes.

Garden Meditation:
An Inner Scrutiny

PRE-MEDITATION

If you do this meditation with a group, ask them to
make a list afterward. The list may include things that
need to be overcome or renewed in the world, in society,
in the community, and in themselves. Discuss the lists
and form them into a litany.

THE MEDITATION

Picture yourself in the most beautiful garden you have
ever seen, filled with trees, bushes, tulips, daffodils, and
all your favorite flowers. It's morning, the start of a new
day. Birds sing, squirrels play, and you can hear the
splash of water from a fountain. Sunshine falling on
your head and shoulders gives you a pleasant warmth. In
this garden, all is peace and harmony. You feel rested,
calm, at peace. It feels good to be here in this safe, secure
place.

This garden is a little taste of the world as God created
it: beautiful, harmonious, happy. It's an image of an
inner garden, a beautiful place inside you where God
wants to meet you, talk to you, listen to you. Meeting
God in your inner garden is one of the ways God will
transform you into a new being, the most wonderful self
you can possibly become. In this garden you will always
find a friend, a healer, a helper, a guide. In this inner
garden you can touch the very source of life, the One

who made you and loves you. Praise God for this inner garden, for all gardens, for all that is wonderful in creation.

From this safe, secure place, resting in God's love, you can look for a little while at some of the problems that have crept into creation that need solving. There are evils, ills, discords, and other harmful things that undermine God's creation of love and harmony.

God created people to be loving, ethical, moral, and just and to share and care for one another. When people behave otherwise, peace and harmony are destroyed. Picture a screen in front of you, blank and white. Ask God to show you some world problems that need overcoming so that you and others can live as God's people. What causes pain and injustice? What disrupts peace and hinders love? See what appears on your inner screen. Gather up what you see in a prayer, a cry to God for help.

Focus again on the screen and come closer to home. Look at our American society and at your own city, town, community. Do evils exist that pull people back from living as God intends: in justice, peace, and happiness? What undermines faith and love? What evils need overcoming in our own communities? Gather these up in a prayer, a petition to God.

Focus once more on the screen. Come closer to home and ask God to reveal in your human nature what needs help, what needs overcoming, so you can grow into your best possible self. We all have hindrances. Look at your inner screen and listen—to learn what God wants to teach you right now, to see ways in which God wants you to overcome barriers to love and growth. Is there any positive action God wants you to take now? Is there any person or group that needs your help? Be open to God's voice in your heart.

Focus on the garden again, seeing all the beauty there. Think of God's goodness in earthly gardens. Think of the garden within you, where God's Spirit speaks to you, where you can always find a friend. Thank God for listening to your needs and for helping you overcome ills and evils; for always offering creative solutions; for blessing you; for making you, if you are willing, a channel of blessing in the world.

Thank God for everything in your inner garden and in your life that is beautiful, lifegiving, and good. Continue to thank God, and when you have finished, quietly open your eyes.

3. Journey to Healing

THE MIND AND HEALING

A profound connection exists between healing and the inner state of mind, heart, and spirit. This mind/body connection is becoming apparent to modern physicians as they increase their knowledge about inner stress as it relates to physical illness.

This concept may be older than you think. Before observing modern discoveries, first let us meander among some ancient myths that show intuition about this connection. (A myth embodies major intuitive insights of a people. It may or may not have historical roots. If the story actually happened, it was preserved because of its significant insight.) The first myth, the tale of Gilgamesh, is important because it is the earliest epic poem on record.[1]

In this parable of inner journey, the Mesopotamian King Gilgamesh, seeks the magic herb with the secret of healing and eternal life. It lies at the bottom of the sea, and Gilgamesh has to dive into the depths to claim this precious prize. Waters of ocean and sea often symbolize the mysterious, unconscious mind (a theme that will recur in these reflections). Gilgamesh's search for the herb of healing symbolizes the human search for God present within the deepest self.

As Gilgamesh begins his quest, he takes up a friendship with Enkadu, at times a treacherous and evil figure. Enemies at first, they eventually become friends and clash with the gods. Enkadu is killed by the gods for his presumptions. It is then that Gilgamesh begins to search for healing and eternal life.

This most ancient of myths tells us how well ancient people knew, instinctively and from experience, about a source of healing and life deep within the psyche. The Greek doctor Hippocrates knew, and many modern physicians agree, that the body itself has healing powers with "state of mind" as a factor. While your conscious mind plays a role, your unconscious mind is crucial, especially when you've experienced hurt, guilt, or wrongdoing.

In Gilgamesh's time (third millennium B.C.), gods were considered external beings who interacted with and controlled humans. They were the unseen forces that caused events beyond even a king's control: weather, seasons, harvest success or failure, health or illness. Not only were gods externalized, early intuitions about inner healing were also externalized in myths and symbols such as the magic herb sought by Gilgamesh.

Although the legend almost divinizes him, Gilgamesh is considered an historic king. As a king, his court, priests, scribes, wise men, and poets had more leisure than other members of the society. They had time to probe into the meaning of death, healing, and life. Which wise man had the insight to suggest the existence of a healing herb? Which poet, tuned to inner realities, turned the inner quest into an outer, mythical journey? The insight that sources of healing and life lie within is aptly captured in the poem. Contemporary scientific concepts were not available to such early thinkers, but they were already onto some spiritual truths to which we can give credence.

Advanced health research verifies the relationships between mind, heart, and body. According to the poem, Gilgamesh went on an external journey. His journey became a myth, a symbol of how things are in our inner world. In modern times, an inner journey is still often a prelude to healing. When you touch your inner source of life through meditation, reflection, prayer, examination of dreams, or active imagination, you release energies for healing and winning. Both ancient myth and modern discoveries support a mind/body relationship that you can use to your advantage.

The myth in the last chapter also supports this connection. I drew a parallel between Tobiah's surfacing of the threatening fish and the facing of inner threats. Both have healing consequences.

The Tobiah story is happier than that of Gilgamesh. His family abides by moral and ethical standards with charity and care for others. He accepts readily a guide, a friend for the journey. Raphael's heavenly origins identify him as a symbol of inner guidance. (He is similar to an inner Angel of Knowing. More about this angel in chapters five and six.) Tobiah might well credit his upbringing for his inner angel, who eventually helps Tobiah overcome dangers and find success, happiness, and healing. There is justice in a son bringing healing to the father who gave him an advantaged, ethical upbringing.

If you compare the story of Gilgamesh with that of Tobiah, you will find in the latter an enormous improvement in spiritual subtlety and understanding. The value of charity and moral living is stressed as a prelude to spiritual journeys. The theme of liberation from evil appears allied with healing, a reminder of the Exodus journey to freedom recounted by Tobiah's people. Relationships play a more important part in Tobiah's story than in Gilgamesh's. Gilgamesh had only one strong relationship (and a questionable one at that) with Enkadu.

Tobiah is part of a close-knit family, with strong ties to even distant relatives. He looks for and accepts a guide, who in turn helps him avoid the pitfalls of the journey and achieve far more success than he anticipated. While Raphael symbolizes the inner guide to whom people should become attuned, he also symbolizes the external human helps, the friends, the spiritual directors people should equally seek out and hear. Good friends help people overcome the serious inner dragons and find their own inner secret of healing and eternal life.

JESUS AND HEALING

Journey-to-healing stories do not stop in the Hebrew Bible. The New Testament authors speak of Jesus as one sent from God. They give as one of his greatest credentials his power to heal as no man ever healed before. In the Bible and in Christian tradition, Christ's life is seen as a journey from heaven to earth to help humans. But the latter portion of his life has the greatest import; it takes him through death and back to heaven. This wins for everyone what Gilgamesh vainly sought: the secret of healing and of eternal life.

Jesus returned to those he left behind, as all heroes do, to bring them the great prize. To fully bestow the gift, he made one last ascending journey to heaven. From there he sent the gift of God's Spirit that enables his followers to make their own journeys, so they may also bring the boon to others as teachers, healers, and bearers of life.

READY FOR HEALING

Two such healers can be found in the third chapter of Acts.[2] Peter and John witnessed the death and resurrection experience, and they received the Holy Spirit at Pentecost. Now they are going up to the Temple to pray. They take the scenic route through the entry called the Beautiful Gate. (Beauty and prayer are two good approaches to healing that are often overlooked.) At this gate lies a man crippled since birth who begs from those who pass. He hopes to get some money from Peter and John, who turn their full attention on him ("Peter fixed his gaze on the man; so did John"). Notice that Peter asks for the man's full attention by saying, "Look at us." The more famous words follow: "I don't have silver or gold, but what I have, I give you! In the name of Jesus Christ the Nazorean, walk!"

In addition to speaking to the man, Peter takes forceful action. He reaches down and pulls the cripple up so that everyone can plainly see. The ex-cripple cooperates by acting on the healing—jumping about and praising God.

Although almost everyone has areas in which they need help, few are ready and willing to receive that help. The cripple's quick response reveals how open and ready he was for his healing. Even his location—by a gate, a place of passage—is a symbol of his yearning for transformation. He also lived in close proximity to beauty and prayer, both gateways to God.

Sometimes using beauty is the best, even the only, way to begin to touch and heal a badly hurt person. (I'm not talking about someone hurt by a physical accident; I'm referring to people hurt in the mind, heart, or spirit, who suffer psychological imbalance, depression, or maladjustment.) Therapist friends have observed that a high, beautiful note from a musical instrument is sometimes the only way to reach autistic children. From the records of friends who are art, dance, and music therapists, I see proven healing effectiveness. The arts facilitate inner journeys, even for children and people struggling with serious brokenness. One of my favorite bumper stickers reads: Art Therapy—Draw from Within.

In addition to beauty, relationships are also important to healing. In the story of the cripple, the man has friends who carry him to the gate each day, and he is not afraid to enter into a new relationship when it is offered by Peter and John. Relationships are important to the apostles, too, as they give the cripple their full attention and ask the same in return. The journey to healing is not a casual matter; it demands total concentration.

The cripple gives Peter and John his total attention as requested, then steps out in faith. He also quickly crowns his healing with praise for its source: the Lord.

A CHECKLIST FOR INNER HEALING

The cripple's story provides a good checklist for times when you or your people need healing.

☐ Are you/they in proximity to places of beauty, prayer, praise, and worship? Are you/they open, ready for change, for transformation?

☐ Do you/they respond to healing invitations with full attention?

☐ Are you/they ready to take practical action and step out in faith?

☐ Are you/they ready to be grateful, to give thanks with enthusiasm and joy?

The story of the beggar offers further reflection for contemporary seekers of wisdom. The beggar was passive at first, but isn't everyone? All humans start out in infancy and childhood completely dependent on others. However, the time comes when another calls forth our gifts and invites us to action, as did the apostles. All who follow a spiritual and moral path, may identify with these apostles, who, through faith, become bearers of life and healing. Here is a checklist for your development as a healer:

☐ Are you, as were the apostles, alert to the needs of others and ready to share your gifts?

☐ Are relationships and others' needs important?

☐ Do you give people your full attention, especially when they are hurting and in need?

☐ Is the healing of people more important than silver and gold? Is the spiritual journey more important than hard cash? Are you willing to spend for the treasure that lies buried in your inner fields?

☐ Do you make time and space for personal prayer, environmental beauty, and public, "temple" ritual and worship in unity with others?

You may not become such a phenomenal healer as Peter, but you do have some capacity worth developing. When it is activated, healing signifies life, God present in a person or community. Interest in this side of healing is increasing, and many gifted leaders are appearing.

CONTEMPORARY HEALERS

Two leaders in healing are the Linn brothers, Dennis and Matthew, both Jesuit priests.[3] They take people on inner journeys into their own past, through guided meditations, to release them from buried hurts and angers. The result is often a physical or emotional healing—sometimes both. I experienced this during a healing retreat, when I dealt with a buried hurt that surfaced like Tobiah's fish. Immediately afterward, I discovered an increased capacity for creative productivity in my art and writing, far more than what was previously possible. I also found myself able to be more of a healing presence to others. I am grateful for these gifts that have enriched me and enabled me to help others.

Aristide Bruni is a priest of the Roman Catholic Consolata Fathers and another leader who guides people on inner journeys toward healing. He intersperses his meditations with songs and often precedes them with a Mass or service. This draws people together and brings them to a greater awareness of God. During the course of everyday life, minds and hearts become cluttered with concern for the mechanics of living. Fr. Bruni's meditations clear away all that, and the wonderful healing presence of God becomes forcibly felt.

When I attended one of his services, I was utterly exhausted by the demands of preparing for it as well as fulfilling numerous other responsibilities at my place of work. "If it only helps the people who come; if only they like it," I thought, along with the inevitable anxiety, "I hope they come."

They did come, in numbers. They received help, and so did I. Not too long into the meditation, I became aware

46

that I was no longer exhausted; rather, I felt wonderful, filled with light, energized, elated by an overwhelming sense of God's presence. "All life, all good things begin from within," said Fr. Bruni, and he spoke of seeds, roses, babies. I added poems and paintings. We meet God within ourselves; that is where healing begins, and that is where Fr. Bruni helped us to travel.

As many people together find the inner place where we encounter God, the sense of God's presence in and around us becomes powerful. We meet within ourselves the Creative Presence that goes far beyond ourselves, that transcends us and our world. When that happens, there may be external as well as internal manifestations. For example, as Fr. Bruni and other leaders pray over individuals, the power of God's presence sometimes becomes so overwhelming that many people fall to the ground in the phenomenon known as being "slain in the Spirit." When this happens, the person rests blissfully in the presence of God for a while.

PHYSICAL AND SPIRITUAL DIMENSIONS

At a retreat near Albany, New York, I met a woman who had experienced this kind of presence several years earlier. As a leader prayed over her, she sensed "a kind of electricity" run through her body, which affected an epileptic condition that had troubled her since childhood. After this experience, she tried going without medication (under a doctor's care). At the time I met her, this woman claimed complete freedom from seizures.

Other people have claimed to be healed during this kind of experience, though I mention them with caution. Medical care is also a miracle and gift from God. You should always care for your body in such common-sense ways as eating right, resting, and taking prescribed medicine when necessary. These down-to-earth measures should never be overlooked. However, a spiritual dimension to health does exist, and it is real, powerful, and available. Healings that take place in dramatic ways, such as being "slain in the Spirit," help some people to become more aware of our inner sources of healing. The dramatics are far less important than the inner state of openness and receptivity to God that they symbolize. Focus on God is what's most important.

LOURDES: THE CLASSIC JOURNEY TO HEALING

Focus on God, openness, and receptivity are also at the heart of pilgrimages to the healing shrine at Lourdes.[4] For those who travel there in search of cures, the externals of the trip and the internal state of mind are linked. Think of the inner changes that occur in a hurting person as friends and family rally round to prepare for such an extensive trip. Think of the arrival at a place where thousands gather. Think of the intensity of hope and religious fervor that builds. People leave their ordinary circumstances and go to an environment where faith is foremost. There are Masses, processions, hymns, and prayers. Everything else falls into the background as God and his power to heal comes into sharp focus. His healing power is everywhere, but on such a pilgrimage people become more open and receptive, so that the power begins to work for them.

Sometimes healings that take place through such pilgrimages are direct, more obviously "miraculous." The epileptic no longer needs her medicine and never has another seizure; the cripple throws away his crutches and dances. More often, however, the inner experience leads to healing in partnership with external, physical means.

MIND/BODY CONNECTIONS

I know of one case in which a pilgrimage journey led to knowledge of a physical cure that worked. In 1952, Bill Schickel, an artist, was stricken with stomach cancer and told he had only a year to live. His family went on a pilgrimage to the shrine of St. Ann to pray for him. En route, on the train, they met someone who spoke of Max Gerson, a New York doctor with a reputation for effecting cancer cures through a radical change in diet. Under Dr. Gerson's regime, Bill had a complete remission.

Dr. Gerson effected many remissions of life-threatening illnesses by changing the body chemistry through diet. His patients lived on high-enzyme, detoxifying vegetable juices. Since that time, carrots, cruciferous vegetables such as cauliflower, cabbage, Brussels sprouts, and broccoli have been shown to prevent cancers through long-range studies by prestigious American institutions including Sloan, Kettering, and John Hopkins. While Bill and the many people who cared about him prayed, they also took practical, physical steps to overcome the illness. The first step, however, was an inner insight.

Interest in the relationship between mind and body, psyche and health, is growing at present through the success of some physicians who have incorporated meditation and imagery into their healing process. Dr. Bernie Siegel's best seller, *Love, Medicine, and Miracles,*[5] has done much to foster knowledge and awareness. He builds on the work of Dr. Hans Selye[6] and the Simontons: Carl, a cancer specialist, and his wife, Stephanie, a psychologist.[7] The successful work of these and other doctors has become so popular that it became the subject of a TV drama, *Leap of Faith,* broadcast over CBS on October 6, 1988.

The books written by these doctors speak powerfully for themselves, so I will say no more than that they reinforce the thesis of this chapter and book: A profound relationship exists between body and spirit. Inner journeys to our hidden wisdom often result in physical as well as mental, emotional, and spiritual healing.

Because this book emphasizes inner journeys to our hidden wisdom, I explore more carefully the inner side of healing. Problems may more often be addressed in terms of psychic and spiritual needs, with fewer references to physical problems, though both areas are related. What you eat and how you care for and respect your body ultimately affect your mental and spiritual state. In turn, inner experiences and attitudes affect your body chemistry. When you are sick or distressed, all areas need examination.

DIFFERENT AREAS OF HEALING

Before ending this chapter, some distinctions between different areas of healing must be made. Although physical, mental, and spiritual needs are interconnected, it helps to pinpoint your main need when you are hurting. When you need healing, into which of the following areas would you classify your need?

The Physical — Is there bodily sickness, pain, or injury? Are there natural ways a healing can take place, such as through better diet or exercise, or is medicine or surgery required? What is going on with your chemistry, your cells, your systems, your organs? What is at the root of your symptoms?

The Spiritual — Is there inner pain due to sin, guilt, wrong choices, selfishness, lack of responsibility, or refusal to grow? Do you need to either receive or give forgiveness and reconciliation? Do you need to alter your attitude? Do you need an ability to act in more loving and creative ways? Do you have a sensitive conscience, a sense of moral values, an ability to love, and a capacity to care for others? Can you see yourself as valuable and loved? Can you see yourself in relation to others, to God, to life?

The Emotional — Do you experience pain or depression resulting from an imbalance or a malformation that is not necessarily your fault? Are there hurts from the past that need healing before you can go forward? Is there brokenness or guilt resulting from the sins of others (as in child abuse) or unjust and chaotic systems?

The Attitudinal — Do you have false or distorted ideas and outlooks that cause you to miss the mark? Do you carry on an inner dialogue that is negative, defeating, frustrating, and that needs to be turned around? Are you limited, hurt, confused, by lack of a positive outlook and a clear, hopeful vision?

The Volitional — Do you possess a desire for healing? How badly? Are there payoffs to being ill? Are you more safe and secure, or do you collect emotional rewards, if you remain sick? Are you ready to be healed?

It's hard to distinguish these categories as they are so interrelated. However, it helps to know which are to the fore at any given time. Bill Schickel needed to make some physical changes in his diet and lifestyle. A woman cheating on her husband needs spiritual and attitudinal healing. Many abused children need to spend hours with a psychologist before the brokenness mends.

On both the physical and psychic levels, some sort of pain, discomfort, or dis-ease reveals a need for healing. The volitional questions are often prompted by a crisis of some kind, which is the subject of the next chapter. While comforts may lull you, crises get you moving. You may not appreciate them while you are in them, but later reflection often shows that a crisis was the beginning of a journey to healing, growth, and expanded life.

Pilgrimages to people and places of healing help you find cures for the ills, the brokenness, the hurts, and the pain that you suffer in the different areas of your life. The best help is to make time for putting aside the accumulation of thoughts, feelings, and concerns with which you manage life. Then you can touch the source of life. You are never far from this source, from God's healing power. It is only a journey away, and the most important place you travel is deep within your own self.

A Meditation for Healing

PRE-MEDITATION

This meditation is akin to one I experienced at a workshop for people with life-threatening illness. While most of my own illnesses have been less serious, I have experienced the power of healing meditation for a few physical disabilities: allergies, rheumatoid knee, a tongue growth that disappeared while I meditated.

Visualizations have a statistical track record for helping people work toward healing, according to Dr. Bernie Siegel, his mentors the Simontons, and others. In many cases, people with cancer have seen results by visualizing their white cells—T cells or other cells designated to fight off threats—as powerful agents, hunters, or warriors organized to battle weak, chaotic, confused cancer cells. Drawings of such visualizations or of dreams help healers such as Dr. Siegel better understand and deal with the nature of their patient's problem.

Fr. Aristide Bruni takes a different approach, guiding people to accept and love everything, even the cancer. A loving attitude in itself is healing. Acceptance opens you up to the good in situations. Bruni also works with the powerful image of light, which is a focus of the meditation that follows.

Traditionally, light is a symbol of God. Many healers work with this image. You may wish to use the name of

God, or Creator, or Jesus, or Healing Spirit, or any others that you're comfortable with as the source of this healing light.

The meditation that follows is not intended to be a substitute for medical attention or lifestyle changes that may be necessary for healing. However it is a powerful adjunct to therapy on many levels.

Sit in a comfortable chair or lie down on a firm surface. Relax by addressing each part of the body, asking it to relax for you. If necessary, take time to tense, then relax the different muscle groups. See the Appendix for a further description of relaxation techniques.

THE MEDITATION

Become as relaxed and comfortable as you can. Take a few deep breaths and close your eyes. Imagine yourself in a place where you feel safe, secure, and happy. Picture your surroundings as peaceful and beautiful. Use your inner senses to visualize it. What do you see? Are there any sounds? Any pleasant smells? In your imagination, reach out to touch something soft and pleasant.

This is your secure spot, your special place of healing. It is a place of warmth and light. A healing light permeates this place. Picture the light shining down on you, warming you, filling your entire body with well-being.

Breathe deeply. With every intake of breath, draw in more healing light. With every exhalation, breathe out any toxins, poisons, or threats to your body.

Breathe in light; breathe out illness.
Breathe in love; breathe out resentment.
Breathe in forgiveness; breathe out grudges.
Breathe in peace; breathe out anger.
Breathe in happiness; breathe out sadness.
Breathe in love and feel yourself filled with love,
surrounded by love; filled with light, surrounded by
light.

Now focus on an area of your body most in need of healing. If you wish you may place your hand there. Feel the healing light gathering there, focusing in that place, driving out illness, restoring health.

As the healing light radiates in you, picture that bodily part working as it should—all the cells, all the muscles doing their job with energy and dispatch.

Rest a little longer in the healing light. Be open to any thoughts, feelings, images, or words that come to you. Thank the healing light. Know that you can return to this healing place and bathe in the healing life again. When you return to your external life, you will feel refreshed and energized. Sense again this beautiful, peaceful place. Say good-bye for now, and quietly open your eyes.

POST-MEDITATION

Write down the thoughts and feelings that came to you during this meditation. Draw the images and visualizations. Discuss these with your doctor or therapist with a supportive group or friend. Explore these words and images for any further clues that might help you heal. They may reveal information about the root of the problem.

4. Journey Through Crises

CRISES KEEP YOU GOING

Journeys in search of healing and wisdom are often precipitated by an urgent need, a lack of an essential, a crisis, even a disaster. In the Tobiah story, there is an economic crisis (Tobit needs his money) and a physical crisis (Tobit's blindness). Tobiah's battle with the fish may be seen as a psychological crisis, and the demon that plagues Sarah may be seen as a spiritual crisis. Many demons frustrate human relationships, especially those between husbands and wives. Both before and during Tobiah's journey, crises seem to keep things moving along.

Crises are a part of your life, too, and they are often what keep you moving and growing, searching and discovering, when comfortable success would allow you to remain complacent. Crises turn up the heat, put on the pressure, and give you the opportunity to expand, transform, or fall apart. In my own case, I usually do a little bit of each.

There are ways to avoid crises. Meditation, inner journeys, responsibility, and careful decisions will keep you growing with fewer disasters, and they will also help you when crises strike again.

The previous chapter pointed out how your healing needs vary. So, too, do the crises in your life. Healing is the necessary result of some crises (illnesses). Other ways of resolving crises involve learning, growth, and expansion as a human being.

DISEQUILIBRIUM IN LEARNING

Any learning process includes cycles of disequilibrium and imbalance that motivate you to work toward knowledge, mastery, and a state of equilibrium in a certain area. However, the learning process expands your mental and/or physical capacities so that you find new challenges, new possibilities, and new problems that put you back into disequilibrium.

For example, a six year old who can't read and begins to see the need is in a state of disequilibrium. After much work, practice, defeat, and victory, he masters reading and achieves equilibrium. But with mastery and maturity, more challenges lie ahead. More interesting stories will beckon, with knowledge waiting to be mined at ever-deepening levels. He will continue in cycles of equilibrium and disequilibrium as he moves on; Tolstoy, Kant, Kierkegaard are waiting to be discovered.

All this does not usually happen in a nice, even flow; most often the cycle is interspersed with joy, pain, and strain before any gain. In most normal human endeavors, and in balance with some success, these challenges keep you motivated and moving.

DISCIPLINE AND SUCCESS

My father, Milton, came of age and founded a family during the Depression, so he was unable to attend college. "I was educated in the school of hard knocks," he often said. With my Uncle Ken and my grandfather, he owned and ran a print shop called the Brooklyn Press. Many nights we missed him at home because he had to be at the shop for an important run. "If one of us isn't there, they could run off thirty thousand mistakes," he would say. I could imagine the crises, the painful experiences that led to this degree of responsibility. We missed him and he missed us, but with a customer waiting for a perfect product, even Mom's good cooking, his living room easy chair, and the radio (including *The Lone Ranger*) had to wait.

This kind of discipline often forestalls crisis. In his book *The Road Less Traveled*, Scott Peck points out that delayed gratification is an important part of education and upbringing.[1] Children who learn how to delay their gratification—to study, for example, when they would rather watch TV—are the ones who grow up responsible. They are able to become successful and find, in the long run, more happiness and reward in life. The right amount of adversity advances human development at all stages.

I have had a healthy dose of adversity, especially as I struggled with the arts. One of my college degrees in is printmaking, and I went through some of my own "hard knock" education to get it. In printmaking, you can work with the most exciting design, the most pure and inspired expression of an idea, but let a few technical details slip by and you end up with a mess. Runs of silkscreen taught me to stop immediately if it wasn't perfect, even though it meant going up to my elbows in paint and thinner with a ten- minute scrub to get a clean screen. That tiny blot on the border wouldn't go away by itself; it would only get bigger unless I got rid of it. Perfect printing means constant vigilance.

My growth as a printmaker meant responsibility on many levels: expressing authentic ideas and feelings, creating an integral visual design, and working carefully in the framework of the craft. Like my father, I learned the hard way. I grew in a craft, was transformed from dabbler to competent craftsperson, and most of it came through crisis.

LOSS, CRISIS, AND GROWTH

Often the difficulties you encounter force you not only to grow, but more importantly, to transform. "Trouble never leads you where it finds you," says Robert Schuller as he explains the second beatitude.[2] Growth, like birth, is not the easiest part of life, but one of the most rewarding.

You will bump into crisis—and opportunity for growth—again and again on your life's journey. At each stage of growth, you press on to gains but also suffer losses. Great opportunities await a baby as she comes into the world, but she leaves behind a warm, sheltered place where she was once completely, comfortably, happily at one with Mother. The new situation may at first appear unwelcoming with its lights, noise, and wide open spaces. The birth is accompanied by the crisis of labor then a smack on the behind. No wonder Baby's first reaction is usually a healthy howl!

This is only the beginning: she goes through crisis at each stage of life[3]: the loss of childhood for the trauma of puberty; the loss of independence and freedom for the responsibilities of work and family; the loss of children as they leave the nest; the loss of loved ones throughout life; finally, the loss of work and sometimes health in old age.

CRISES AND MOLECULES: A HIGHER LEVEL

Face it, crisis accompanies most of your growth. However, if it weren't for these traumas, you might never reach your full potential. Most often, a crisis forces you to struggle toward more growth, greater responsibility, and higher awareness.

You can find many examples of crisis/growth and transformation throughout history, life, and literature. Conflict is the stuff of novels, stories, and TV dramas. Nature itself provides you examples, right down to the molecular level. Ilya Prigogine,[4] winner of the 1977 Nobel Prize in chemistry for his work in nonequilibrium thermodynamics, applied what happens on a molecular level to human and sociological levels. The mystery of transformation through crisis seems to pervade all of life.

In the past, with a more static, Aristotelian concept of the universe, change was seen as a matter of cause and effect. People sometimes thought of God as the "unmoved mover" who created everything like a great machine with interrelated parts. Once God gave that first push, things kept humming along. Picture a game of pool, for example. You hit a ball with the cue; it hits others balls and sets them in motion. Cause and effect.

In days past, the cue, balls, pockets, and table were considered solid material, made of matter. With the discovery of the atom, scientists began to realize that these objects are not so solid after all. There is more space than matter in atoms, and even the massive pool table is a whirling world with far more space than solid. It is an open system in which tiny particles of matter exist in a larger flow of energy.

Ilya Prigogine's theory of dissipative structures points to the role of stress in transforming these open systems. When a system is placed under increasing stress, it holds together (maintains its equilibrium). But when the stress becomes too great, disequilibrium occurs. The original structure falls apart, disintegrates. However, the atoms work to reorganize themselves so that they come together at a higher level. By this quantum leap into a new structure, a new and more integrated configuration occurs. For example, metal that is heated, hammered, and plunged into cold water becomes stronger and has more visual glint and energy after this formative crisis.

Even systems on the molecular level seek harmony, balance, transformation, and growth. The end result of a crisis can be a higher level of organization. In thermodynamics, energy is never lost, only transformed, and this process of reorganization allows many useful functions to occur; homes are heated and engines are powered. Prigogine's thermodynamic principles also extend to such fields as sociology, city planning, and ecology.

CRISES AND COMMUNITY

Physical evolution is related to those same principles of transformation and growth through stress. Picture the primal seas in which individual microbes swim, feeding and multiplying until they outnumber their food sources. What a crisis! The system isn't working anymore. What will happen? The microbes grow into a new, more integrated configuration. They unite into cells, then into even larger organisms that make more efficient use of the available food. Different cells begin to perform different functions. New organisms are born on a higher, more complex level.

How many times has getting together to work with others solved serious problems? Of course I wasn't around when it happened in those primeval seas, but I've seen it occur on personal, family, and community levels. Crisis and concern have often transformed a group of individuals with cross-purposes into a cooperating community.

CRISES AND CHOICE

When a crisis confronts you, you have a crucial advantage that molecules don't have: You have a choice in how you're going to react. At your higher stage of consciousness, the growth for the better does not happen automatically; you have to choose it. In any crisis, you have the choice either to grow and expand your present parameters or to become bitter, angry, chaotic, limited, even destroyed by the threat.

Your decision to choose growth is not absolute. Some people are brought up in more affirming and hopeful circumstances; others are reared in less favorable circumstances, deprived of love, education, or material needs. Some are even victims of abuse and outright malice. The latter groups may find choosing growth much more difficult. Relative as choices may be, you can still choose the more hopeful, life-giving, expanding response to crisis. Your decision will be much easier if you are lucky enough to have made inner journeys.

Take comfort in the thought that you are not alone in your struggles to survive and grow. The dawn of life on this planet came through crisis. And if cells can do it, so can you. Plus, you have much more help. God is present to you, ready to guide your inner wisdom, your unconscious awareness. Something deep and powerful inside you encourages your growth, healing, wholeness, transformation, and success.

If you learn how to draw on your inner resources, you will find the answers, the help, the strength to see you through all difficulties, all possible crises. Your inner wisdom can turn the worst to good. This may not be apparent at first. You have to take time to journey to that secret inner place where the Holy Spirit keeps you in unity with God. In the book of Revelation,[4] Jesus says, "Behold, I stand at the door and knock." Jesus speaks for God's life source, present within each of God's children. He promises to sup with they who open the door. This secret inner place is where that door is open, where that nourishing table is spread. It is the place to go to find transformation, harmony, order, and cosmos in whatever threatens.

It might take time, especially at first. Your human feelings, your hurts may be so strong that you need to work through them while your healing and ordering forces take shape. You might have to discern which areas of healing (as described in the previous chapter) need special attention. You might also need the help of others.

Often, an ache or pain indicates your need for healing. The symptom starts you on a search for the right doctor, the right medicine, the right counselor. You sense disequilibrium, distress, imbalance, inner assault, something out of order. You need to find the area (or areas, for they usually overlap) to work on and the routes to take to solve the problem(s).

The road to healing is so often filled with crisis that we even speak of "the healing crisis," the high pitch of fever that may determine whether a patient lives or dies. The threat is great, but so is the opportunity to overcome.

The Chinese character for "crisis" is the same as that of "opportunity." In ordinary life, the biggest crisis often gives you the biggest opportunity, pushes you toward the greatest growth, increased responsibility, and personality development. Many people launch into an emotional, prayerful, problem-solving, or work fever to save the day and find they have gone beyond previously narrower limits. You grow and expand through crisis—unless you become bitter, angry, and even narrower than you were before.

When your feelings are in chaos, when things seem a mess, it's time to quiet down, to meditate, so that the door to that secret place can open, so that you can hear the gentle whisper of wisdom. Then your creative forces come through and begin the hopeful, ordering, problem-solving process that will save the day. You will know what to do, whom to consult. Staying in tune during difficult times will not only help you find the best solution but will also help you use the problems to grow and transform.

DEATH

The biggest crisis, the one that may seem to preclude further growth and transformation, is the death of a loved one. I recently went to see a dying friend and found the experience to be other than what I expected.

Elaine was a black woman with a beautiful voice. She had given many people happiness with this gift, but now her voice was a whisper and her words came slowly and painfully. A rare form of palsy resulted in paralysis, which kept her head tilted back at an odd angle, and she could walk only with people's assistance. Though my heart was heavy for Elaine and I dreaded seeing her in this condition, I went for an overnight visit.

Elaine rested as I sat by her bedside in quiet meditation. Gradually, I became aware of a great beauty in her face, her head, even in her hands. I tried to capture in a drawing some of this incredible luminosity, but to little avail. The beauty was too big; something holy was happening. A diamond, whose brilliance is formed from the pressures of the earth, came to mind.

Elaine had borne many of life's pressures patiently, and now she faced the greatest of all. Her choices had always been loving ones of service and celebration. Before I left, I prayed for her, and she answered, "Amen." With slow, whispered words, she thanked me for praying with her, for coming to see her, and she invited me to return.

Those words and Elaine's beauty meant a great deal to me. As I sat with her, I asked the inevitable question, "Why? Why this pain, this disability, this helplessness?" The strange sense of beauty and sacredness helped me to know that through her biggest crisis, the biggest growth and biggest transformation were in process.

The visit to Elaine brought me closer to her, but it also brought me closer to those who were attending her. I had felt somewhat alienated by differences in areas of politics and religion. These differences seemed far less important in relation to the sacred event that was happening and in relation to the wise and loving care I saw them giving Elaine. A deeper chord of unity was struck. I felt more at home with old friends than I had in a long while. The crisis that transformed Elaine also brought growth and healing to me.

LIKE GOLD IN THE FIRE

Life is risky business, and you can't get too far into it, or even out of it, without meeting crisis. Inner journeys prepare you for your own crises; they may also enable you to guide and help others through theirs. Some of these people may include children, who cope on a less conscious level. They have stress just like adults do, and crises affect all age groups. The need for two working adults in many families and the pace of modern life have put a great deal of pressure on everyone. Stress management workshops have become one of the signs of our times.

No one can escape some difficulty in life, and most people have much more than they want. Having a positive outlook and knowing what to do alleviates the negative potential. When problems are unavoidable, it helps to know that people under stress are diamonds in the making. Diamonds and other precious gems form over a period of time under enormous stress. Gold becomes precious only when it is tried by fire. Have you heard the expressions "a diamond in the rough" and "a perfect jewel" applied to people? Human faith is often "tried by fire" like gold. It is in your times of difficulty, accepted and worked through, that you are most transformed.

An oft-repeated premise of this book is: When you meet and overcome the dragons you find within, you have more resources to overcome external dragons and difficulties. Valuable knowledge about your inner dragons is available from two sources, the discoveries by modern psychologists, and the ancient wisdom found in religious symbols. The next section of this book will explore some of these, in some cases juxtaposing the two. A brief synopsis of concepts and images derived from Carl Gustav Jung focuses special attention on the structures of the psyche. A picture of the tension and balance of your inner world, both conscious and unconscious, helps you to work with them for healing, growth, and good. These dynamic energies, richly symbolized in art and scripture, illustrate why many stressful situations arise and how they can be resolved. The overall picture is positive and hopeful.

Morning Star Meditation

PRE-MEDITATION

The symbol of the morning star is so rich that it offers many meditation possibilities. I have given this one to mature adults, who found it a source of comfort, renewal, and inspiration.

The book of Revelation describes an angel who arrives to utter words of approval or disapproval to the key Christian communities. Many have interpreted him to be, or to speak for, Jesus, the Christ. In this meditation, you can use Jesus' name, Daystar, God, or Lord. The morning star is promised "to him [her] who overcomes." The morning star that appears in the dawn sky is called "daystar" because it is a signal of the coming day. From early times, "Daystar" was also a title given to the Christ, who is a herald of a new day in the human spiritual journey.

At most times in your life, you have at least a few problems that need solving, overcoming. These sometimes becomes like mountains that threaten to overwhelm you. The promise of the Daystar is that you have help within yourself and beyond yourself to overcome and return to peace.

Do not verbalize the section titles below when giving the meditation to others. They are to help you clarify the themes and, if necessary, to reorganize the meditation to suit the needs of your group.

THE MEDITATION

Picture yourself waking early in the morning while it's still dark. When you retired last night, you had problems on your mind. You were restless with many responsibilities, worries, and cares pressing in on you. Because of these, you woke up earlier than usual. Now sleep eludes you. The house you rest in, quiet and still, is surrounded by a garden. You decide to get up and go outside into the garden.

The Star

As you step through the door, heavy blackness surrounds you. You can barely see the shadows of trees. You know many beautiful and interesting things are in the garden, but right now all of them are hidden. Within you also, it is dark. There are possibilities, promises, and solutions to your troubles, but for now they are hidden. All is still, deathly quiet. Then you look up and see, shining in the darkness, a brilliant diamond of light, a beautiful jewel in the night sky, a forerunner of morning.

New Beginnings

Now you notice around you stirrings of life: the sound of crickets, the rustling and chirping of birds, chipmunks, squirrels. These are sounds of new beginnings, of nature awakening to a new day. You hear laughter coming from a nearby house as children wake up. The human race is also called to begin a new day.

The first rays of the sun begin to tint the eastern sky with a rosy-purplish hue that gradually bathes everything around you in a growing light. All the garden life you love so much—flowers, shrubs, trees—emerge from the darkness, still touched with morning dew. Everything looks and smells and feels so fresh, so new, and it lifts your spirits.

You give to the Creator a quiet "thank you" for the start of new day, for the beautiful creation, for the stirrings of life around you and within you. You feel within yourself stirrings of new life, promise, hope, a fresh beginning to everything you care about. The morning star is bringing you another day, another chance, another opportunity for life, for growth, for love.

The Inner Daystar

The morning star of the sky heralds the coming of day, which overcomes darkness. You also have within you a morning star to help you overcome all that is dark, troubling, evil, destructive, chaotic. God, the Creator, is greater than all darkness, destruction, and death. God is within you, ready to take on all your troubles, all your cares and concerns, to give you the creative solutions, the strengths, by which you can overcome. Give your troubles over to God completely. Tell the Lord about anything on your mind that is troubling you right now.

Listen as your inner daystar tells you to give all your cares and troubles, all that is dark for you right now, to God. God will be the victor in your battle against these troubles and against troubles to come. Listen and let your inner daystar tell you the meaning behind your troubles, what you need to learn right now and what you need to overcome within yourself and within your situation. Let your inner daystar comfort you, assure you. You will be all right. The solutions will come, and through it all you will grow if you stay close to your inner wisdom and God.

Now your troubles are not so big; you feel calm and peaceful, and a flow of understanding washes over you. You will know what to do. You will see the solution at exactly the right time. Even now, some answers are beginning to form in your consciousness. More will come as inevitably as the daystar heralds daytime, as sure as darkness gives way to light, as sure as this new day is dawning.

The Call to Love

This new day comes from God's love. Thank God. Greet God with love. Greet the day with love. Greet all the beauty of creation with love. And the people you will meet this day—family, friends, strangers, good and bad, happy and suffering, rich and poor—resolve to greet them all with love. Right now, plan to give everyone with whom you come in contact today a silent, inner greeting of "I love you." Right now, resolve to speak only good of people. Resolve to put your hand across your mouth and physically stop your words if you're tempted to say something negative about someone. Right now, resolve to greet every problem that comes your way with these words: "There is good in this for me. I will give it over to my Lord. In God, I will overcome."

Thanksgiving

As the garden around you grows brighter and more beautiful in the fresh new day, you know that you also are given new beginnings, new strengths, and new ideas to work out every problem. From darkness emerges a sparkling new hope for you and for the world.

Thank God for new beginnings. Thank God for overcoming for you, in you, with you. Thank God for the hope and promise in the words, "To those who overcome, I will give the morning star." Thank God that this star of hope will rise again for you each day on your earthly journey, until the final victory when you will be with God and all God's people forever and ever. Thank and praise God for the hope He gives. When you are finished, quietly open your eyes.

5. Journey into Consciousness

AN ANGEL OF INNER KNOWING

In the mysterious book of Revelation,[1] a powerful figure appears to the author, John. The figure has hair white as wool and eyes like fire; his feet gleam like polished brass refined in a furnace; his right hand holds seven stars, and a two-edged sword comes out of his mouth. The voice of this awesome being is like the roar of rushing water, and his face shines like the sun at its brightest. It becomes apparent from the text that this startling figure speaks for the Christ, and his awesome appearance seems to say, "Listen and listen well. What I am going to say is of vital importance."

In chapters two and three of this last book in the Bible, the messenger tells of the state of seven churches. These seven churches form a geographic circle, and because a circle symbolizes wholeness we know that the message is for the whole church community at that time. Further, it is a universal message to all the people of God for all time.

Each message begins with the Greek word, "Oida," "I know." Some of the words are sympathetic: "I know your deeds; I know the slander, the sufferings you endure." Other words are stern: "I know the reputation you have of being alive when, in fact, you are dead." Accordingly, affirmations or exhortations, comforts or warnings follow each community's message.

At the end of each letter, the figure gives a powerful promise clothed in symbolic images. "To the one who overcomes, I will give: A crown of life, the hidden manna, the morning star, a white pebble with a new name written on it to be known only by the one who receives it."

What needs overcoming? What constitutes the victory? In past chapters of this book, fear, crisis, and illness were pinpointed as dragons to be overcome, and others remain. Suffice to say that you almost always need to overcome something. Most important to your needs is the available presence of that awesome angelic figure who says "Oida," "I know." That presence knows who you are, what you are enduring or suffering, how and why you are failing, where you have needs, and how those needs may be fulfilled. This knowing presence of light is not beyond you. It is within, the goal and heart of your inner journey.

CONSCIOUS AND UNCONSCIOUS MIND

Some of the knowledge and the promises offered by your inner angel will be examined in these pages to see what you can learn about the journey to become who you really are—your greatest self. You will see links between biblical wisdom and the psychology developed by Carl Gustav Jung. Dr. Jung made an in-depth study of symbols to help him find out more about the inner workings of people.[2] His insights help us to expand and apply the wisdom of scripture, while the resonating biblical signs give greater meaning to what Jung discovered.

The images of scripture speak to two poles of your inner life: the conscious and the unconscious of your mind. Your conscious world of logic and linear reasoning likes to figure things out. It relates, compares, and works to know the reasons for things. Your unconscious mind, too, is always absorbing information. It thinks and feels in imagery and symbols that have many levels of meaning. This unconscious activity affects you powerfully whether or not you are aware of it.

To allow the symbols to speak to your conscious and unconscious alike, linger on each symbol; allow it to speak fully through your senses and imagination before you rush on to find a logical, rational (and more limited) meaning. The symbols activate powerful inner energies, and it's important to experience them fully and deeply on many levels of meaning.

Think of the morning star, one of the symbols the angel refers to in Revelation. Don't rush to ask, "What does it mean?" First, picture yourself waking early in the morning while it's still dark. When you retired last night, you had problems on your mind. You were restless with many responsibilities and woke earlier than usual. Now sleep eludes you. You decide to go outside into the garden.

As you step through the door, heavy blackness surrounds you. Then you look up and see shining in the darkness a brilliant diamond of light, a forerunner of morning. Around you are stirrings of life: birds, chipmunks, and squirrels. A radiance of light rises over eastern hills. The garden begins to take on form and glow in the morning light. Everything around you speaks of new beginnings, of nature awakening to a new day. You also will have a new beginning, new strength, new creativity with which to solve your problems and face your work. From darkness emerges a sparkling new hope for you and for the world.

Now the conscious mind has more experience with which to work. Christian theologians say the morning star represents Jesus, who revealed more about God's being to people. Throughout the Bible, light is always a symbol of God and God's presence. In each individual, time must pass before this understanding, this light, can be absorbed. It gradually dawns.

In more ordinary language, light is a symbol of awareness and understanding. "To shed light on

something" means "to increase conscious awareness."
"She saw the light" means "she was made aware." The
light bulb flashing in a comic character's dialogue
balloon associates light and conscious ideas.

The link between Jesus, the Light, and our human
consciousness becomes more apparent in John's Gospel
references to Jesus as both the Light and as the Word of
God. The word "word" implies a clarity, a light of
consciousness. The Hebrew word for "word" is "dabhar,"
which means "a creativity that brings life into being,
that effects what it says."[3] Like the morning star, Jesus
brings a new awareness, a consciousness, intended to
transform you to your very depths.

The transformation of consciousness has been
seriously explored by modern psychologists, with helpful
results. New discoveries, however, are prefigured by
ancient symbols. These symbols engaged people in their
wholeness so that the "dabhar," the Word, could radiate
into both the conscious and unconscious.

The angel described in Revelation has eyes that burn
with fire. Picture the most alive eyes you ever saw,
observing everything carefully, lovingly, not missing
anything. This mysterious presence has infinite
knowledge, and no part of your being is beyond its range.
Attention to its presence will lead you to wisdom with a
healthy balance between the many forces that constitute
your inner mind. Its presence will lead you to unity
within yourself and with others, people with whom you
come in contact in your external dealings. This presence,
this "Oida" angel, is a creative one, ready and willing to
help you become your greatest self.

JUNG'S INSIGHTS

To look further into how this inner presence creates
and unifies, I want to draw a psychological picture of
what lies within. New names and diagrams help clarify
some of the mysteries of the human psyche. Modern

psychologists also shed light on our inner workings and, in tandem with older traditions, they offer valuable information.

The psychologist Carl Jung gives the most serious outline of the structures of the psyche. In this chapter and in the next, I will share a brief outline, but with precautions.[4] Jung himself was wary of projecting these structures onto any person. He listened carefully to each patient, seeking the secret to each situation. He did not readily label the person or the problem or try to match them with a theory. However, in the course of working with many individuals, Jung discovered elements common to everyone.

This chapter deals with conscious structures and ego. The unconscious is dealt with in the next chapter. It is difficult to make distinctions between the conscious, pre-conscious, and unconscious mind. You are a whole, and all your inner energies are interrelated. However, if you can distinguish between them, you can then understand the wonderful, complex being you are so that you can deal with yourself and others more patiently, lovingly, and realistically.

If you are already familiar with Jung's theory, some of the links between psychology and scripture may still be of interest. And of course it's always good to hear new stories. If you are not familiar with Jung's work, please remember that this is the briefest of outlines. Jung's valuable work deserves further attention. The "Sources and Further Reading" at the end of this book will direct you to some good sources.

Sensate and Intuitive

Jung distinguished three psychic levels: the **conscious**, the **personal unconscious**, and the **collective unconscious**. The conscious is the part of your mind that is directly aware of your surroundings as well as your thoughts, feelings, memories, and imaginings.

The distinction between awareness of what's going on outside and what's going on inside is an important one. You have the ability to be aware of both. However, you can't always pay equal attention to both at the same time. The major thrust of your energy has to focus on one or the other. Sometimes the fascination, beauty, wonder, or danger of the outside world claims your awareness; sometimes your own feelings and thoughts will predominate. The external and the internal comprise one of the many poles, or pairs of opposites, you deal with, either consciously or unconsciously, as you live and grow. For simplicity's sake, let's call the energies that attend the external your **sensate** energies and those that attend the internal your **intuitive** energies.

If you are to be a whole, balanced, healthy person, each pole will need its time and attention. To survive in the world, to be realistic, you need your sensate self. However, to deal with the world, to learn what it has to teach, to see meaning and value, you need your intuitive, reflective self. The intuitive side also keeps you in touch with your unconscious self.

While you need to give time and attention to both your sensate and intuitive sides, you usually prefer (give more time and attention to) one or the other. Some people have a slight preference, giving one side a little more scope, while others have strong preferences, giving one side a great deal of scope. When you give more scope to one side, the other side gets less energy. A strong sensate person may have a weak intuitive side, while a strong intuitive may have a less-developed sensate side. You must understand this important principle, as it affects many more polarities within both the conscious and unconscious of your mind.

People who have balanced sensate and intuitive sides usually have achieved this maturity and wholeness over a period of time, through many experiences and interactions with other people, including their opposites. You may favor one pole, which is fine as long as you tolerate your opposites and appreciate the way you balance each other out. Your awareness of inner structures can help you move toward wholeness within yourself and then reconciliation with others.

Your opposites not only balance you out, they put you in touch with your less-developed energies, enabling you to expand and grow. You may find yourself seeking out your opposite type for a friend, co-worker, or marriage partner. Love thrives on its opposite. You unconsciously know you need the others with their differences. However, the mistake people often make is to try to change the others and make them like themselves. The book *Please Understand Me* was written from observations of the misery this attraction to opposites causes many people.[5]

If you strongly prefer your sensate or intuitive side, you are capable of making great contributions because of your well-developed preference. For example, the highly sensate athlete will excel in some sport, and the highly intuitive poet will write wise verse. But if you have a strong preference, you are also less whole and need the balance of people with the opposite preference or ability in order to function well. Strong intuitives need the realism of sensate partners, friends, co- workers, and family to counterbalance a more inner-oriented personality. Strong sensates need the intuitives' gift of wisdom and insight that gives meaning to external experiences.

Think back to the description of the morning star. The sensate person will appreciate the beauty, look forward to getting up at 4:00 a.m. to see it, check the alarm, put gas in the car, and pack the lunch for a trip that will make the best view possible. However, the intuitive person will find meaning and value in the experience by relating it to human psychology or spirituality and writing a poem or story so that more people can see the meaning.

Thinking and Feeling

According to Jung, the conscious performs the following four functions: thinking, feeling, sensing, and intuiting.

What we've said about the sensate and intuitive energies applies to **thinking** and **feeling**. These functions are also a pair of polar opposites, and you probably favor one over the other. Some people sympathize with people and their needs; others need to figure out why things work the way they do and record the results in an ordered, organized way. Everyone has energies that encompass both functions, but one or the other will predominate at different times. If your energies focus on figuring things out, you are a thinker; if your energies more often focus on valuing, empathy, and emotion, you are a feeler. The stronger one side is, the weaker the other.

You need opposite people to balance you out. The differences between people support varying human needs and enable people to collectively care for all sides of life. Unfortunately, people tend to either love or hate their opposites and often project their own unconscious weaknesses on them. This is one of the dragons of the inner journey, to be dealt with in the next chapter.

Perceiving and Judging

Research has uncovered other factors that affect temperament: **perceiving** and **judging**. Perceivers prize freedom, adventure, excitement, and open-ended situations, which enable them to creatively enjoy and work with life as it happens. Judgers prefer structured, ordered frameworks so they know what to expect as they carefully fulfill responsibilities. Judgers help to maintain institutions that carry out what perceivers originally envision.

Another Pair of Opposites

Interacting with the above six preferences (sensate and intuitive, thinking and feeling, perceiving and judging) is another pair of opposites, **introversion** and **extroversion**. Extroverts are more outgoing, geared to the people around them; introverts respond more to the inner, subjective world. Extroverts are energized by interaction with people and will be more likely to stay at the party all night. Introverts, on the other hand, will enjoy the party a little while, then seek some solitude to recover and recoup their energies. They may interact with people in more reflective ways: keeping a journal of their experiences, writing letters, mentally sorting out what has happened.

When introversion and extroversion combine with the preferences of intuiting/sensing, thinking/feeling, and perceiving/judging, all of which you may experience in different degrees and intensities, you see that you have much about your conscious self to get to know. (And we have yet to talk about your unconscious!)

THE GATEKEEPER EGO

The principle organizer and orchestrator of all this activity is the **ego.** The ego is also called the "gatekeeper" because it decides what to admit into the conscious mind. You experience so much of the outside world each moment, you simply can't cope with all of it; only certain impressions are allowed into awareness. Plus, the unconscious mind is constantly working, but the ego only allows the conscious to be aware of some of it.

The ego allows your conscious to deal with some things and not others, based on your past memories, feelings, impressions, and personality preferences. Some people picture the ego as a distillery refining what is most important and relevant to needs and feeding only that to your awareness. The ego gives your personality its consistency and character.

Usually, unpleasant, hard-to-handle elements that arouse anxiety are kept locked out. But sometimes powerful thoughts, feelings, and experiences override this inner gatekeeper and force themselves into your awareness. This is why life's crises often lead to your greatest growth. Often, prayer, meditation, listening, and reflective study enable you to avoid the crunch and grow in greater peace.

As gatekeeper, the ego wants to maintain relative stability in the conscious. That is why it will try to keep out unfavorable thoughts and feelings. Naturally you feel good when thoughts about yourself are good, so the ego allows more of these impressions to enter. Perhaps that accounts for the words "egotist" and "egomaniac," which are applied to people who have inflated and unrealistic opinions of themselves. This is often compensation for insecure feelings caused by lack of self-esteem. Usually, pointing out faults will only work to strengthen the ego barrier and raise defenses further. Acceptance and non-judgmental listening are more helpful. When people feel genuinely recognized and affirmed, they often are able to drop their ego defenses and look at themselves more realistically.

Acceptance puts the ego at greater ease and allows it to be more open and trusting. While it helps to have acceptance from someone (I recommend trusted spiritual guides and friends) in order to make a successful inner journey, you also grow in self-acceptance through the process itself.

The inner journey reveals friendly inner energies that are ready to help you; in touching the source of life within you, you touch God, the friend above all friends. The self-acceptance that results helps you to better accept others and, often, to be accepted by them in return. This allows the ego to lower its defenses and accept more reality and truth from both external and internal sources.

The ego tries to bar unsettling information. The conscious mind tends to rationalize. Thus, you cannot rely on them as complete sources of truth. Instead, you must go deeper, into the unconscious mind, to draw out a full picture of how things really are. There you will meet the angel of light, who can truly say, "Oida," "I know." Fortunately, this awesome presence says that you are deeply cared for. Your good deeds are seen and approved; your weaknesses and failures are noted so you can overcome them. The light of knowledge and love wants to shine with truth and love in your consciousness and bring more of what is creative and life-giving to your awareness.

One of psychologists' great contributions is their increased knowledge of the power and wisdom in the unconscious. Consciousness is only the tip of the iceberg of what you "know," only a partial regulator of behavior. The discovery of unconscious power, however, should not decrease the grandeur and power of the conscious mind, which is the crowning glory of being human. Its functions and powers assume leadership and command in your inner world. It sets goals, plans, evaluates, explores, delves, and discovers.

In the next two chapters, you will read about individuation, the process of asserting who you really are in order to realize more of your potential to be. Your growth and maturity rest on your conscious eagerness for increased awareness of both outer and inner worlds. Increased awareness of the unconscious serves to provide the conscious mind with more truth and wisdom to work with and more energy for you to pursue what the conscious mind chooses.

New Beginnings Meditation

PRE-MEDITATION

This is a pick-and-choose meditation. I use all three
parts at once with adult groups. However, you can just
use one at a time in shorter time spans. Do not read the
titles as you give the meditations; they are to highlight
the images for your understanding. All three need the
introduction, and part three works best preceded by
parts one and two.

Part One, The Morning Star, may be used for children.
The image is from the Book of Revelation. In Part Two,
you may give the figure a name your group will respond
to best: "Jesus," "Lord," "Wisdom," "Spirit," or another
"image of God's Love" in place of "Prince of Peace."

Part Three, The Children, is for adults only. It was
inspired by a friend's vision, a gift to her and all of us.
After this vision, Lois has gone on to write and tell
stories that enchant and teach children of all ages. I
thank her for sharing her gift.

THE MEDITATION

Introduction: The Seashore

With your faith imagination, picture yourself sitting
on a sandy dune in the early morning while it is still
dark. Though darkness is all about you, you feel at peace
as you gaze out over the calm waters of an ocean that
stretches out into darkness, reflecting the stars.

Recently, you have been in difficulties, and your feelings were like the ocean in a storm. Now you are grateful to be alone, quiet and calm. You are waiting for morning.

Part One: The Morning Star

Suddenly, up above you, you see a bright star, a star that outshines all others: the morning star.

The morning star captures all the newness of fresh starts; it holds all the promise of a new beginning, of another and better day.

As you focus on the star, you hear the sounds of birds waking up and singing. You feel a fresh morning breeze across your face. You smell fresh morning air. From the east, light appears—a deep purple becoming a rosy pink. The clouds, too, light up with color.

The morning star is the first sign of new life, including yours. It carries a message of new beginning. Be quiet in the light of the morning star, and see what gift it brings to help you start anew, fresh, and at peace in God's love.

Part Two: The Prince of Peace

In the dawning light, you see a figure in a white robe walking toward you. The figure reflects the growing, warming light and also radiates a gentle glow. You hold your breath as you realize who it is.

It is the Prince of Peace who smiles at you and embraces you in a great, warm hug. He says, "What was all the turbulence about?"

Think of a time in your life when things seemed very difficult: a time when things did not go right; when you made a mistake; when you hadn't enough time or energy; when there was a misunderstanding; when you thought you wouldn't make it. See the people involved and the place where the turbulence occurred. Feel the feelings. Now feel the Prince's hand rest on your shoulder as he pulls you back into his peace and toward a new beginning. Listen to what he tells you about your problems. Ask questions. Rest awhile in his peace.

Part Three: The Children

The sun rises, a bright and glowing orb over the horizon, and the sky sends forth its glory. The clouds are rose- and gold-colored. The sea gulls sweep across the sky, reflecting all the colors.

You see many small figures approaching you from over the sand dunes and from along the beach. Children are coming to you from all directions. They even come in boats over the water. Some are very small; some are older. But they are all growing; they all hold the promise of new beginnings.

The children gather around you. You feel your love going out to them, and you feel their love coming toward you. Those who are closest reach out to you and stroke your arm. You reach out and touch the silky hair of one and the soft, smiling cheek of another. You receive so much love from them and from the Prince of Peace, who is still with you.

When it is time for the children to go, they scatter over the dunes, waving good-bye, blowing you kisses. The Prince of Peace says, "These are my little lambs. Feed them. These are new beginnings in my people. Nurture these new beginnings; nurture my people."

He continues, "There are new beginnings in you, also. Let me help them to shine forth like the morning star heralding the day. To whoever overcomes, I will give the morning star with new beginnings of life and love."

Listen to the Prince of Peace now as he tells you how he will help you overcome, how he will nurture new beginnings in you and in others. Rest quietly in peace as he speaks to you.

6. Journey to the Unconscious

One of the promises made to "him/her who overcomes" by the angel in Revelation is a gift of "hidden manna." Think of the word "hidden." It suggests a secret, something not readily discernible. In your inner unconscious, you have a secret life that is not readily discerned or used. In this secret place, you are able to encounter God and the hidden presence of God in others. From this source God wants to give you manna, food, nourishment, exactly as you need it on your journey through life.

Manna too, is an image. Most people love food, and everybody needs it. It provides growth to children and strength and energy to people of all ages. No special celebration is complete without food. It is a lifetime source of physical sustenance.

However, the manna in Revelation is sustenance for the Spirit. It reminds people of God's care for the Israelites as they journeyed through the desert en route to the promised land. God asked for their trust and provided for them day by day. Manna also reminds many Christians of the Eucharist, that spiritual food that signifies God's presence to his people.

"Hidden manna" means all this and more. Like your inner Angel of Knowing, it will emerge from your creative unconscious as you make time and space for God through prayer, worship, reflection, and commitment. God wants to give you all that you need for healing, growth, and wisdom. It's worth delving into your hidden world to find this manna so that God can nourish you for all you are meant to do and become.

The manna image represents a hidden side of yourself that lies beneath conscious awareness in your dark or shadow side, your unconscious mind. Don't let the expression "dark side" scare you, because a lot of friendly energy is there waiting to be made conscious so that it can help you.

Remember the ego? Because of it, you can only be conscious of so much at one time. Your memory is capable of storing many bits of information, but you can only recall a few at a time. You have experienced much more that your ego buried deep, and those memories are difficult, if not impossible, to get at. Years of analysis are necessary for some troubled people to uncover buried memories of painful experiences. Some things never reach your conscious awareness. If and when they do, they will probably be enigmatic images with more levels of meaning than your conscious mind can figure out.

This mysterious, hidden part of you has a powerful nature of its own, and it exercises an enormous influence on your life. According to Jung, if you don't face some of your weaknesses, those dragons on your dark side, you automatically **project** them on others. You see your own weakness, confusion, and evil in the other person rather than in yourself where you can contend with it as the "Oida" angel asks. The Nazis are the perfect example of this projection, according to Eric Fromm.[1] They projected their dark side on the Jews, while they saw themselves as supermen. This projection limited their ability to grow and mature in a healthy way. It brought great suffering and tragedy to millions of people, including themselves.

This example of projection happens all the time on a lesser scale. While the grief it causes may not be as great, the projection principle on any level is one of the destructive dragons of the unconscious that brings about many misunderstandings and misery.

Certain traditional religious practices helped people of the past and still help people today deal with their dark sides so they will be less likely to project them on someone else. Jewish people have a season, Elul, followed by High Holy Days, and then a special day of atonement, Yom Kippur, to help them deal with their shadow side. Roman Catholics have the sacrament of reconciliation to help them explore their dark sides. These feasts and sacraments, practiced well, provide a model for all inner journeys, all looks at the dark side. They look within in a communal context, after meditation on God's love and affirmation of them as a people.

Other people have ways to deal with their shadow side. Protestants talk with their ministers less ritually than Catholics but often with greater consciousness and less rote. Moslems fast each Ramadan, the ninth month of each year. Eastern religions favor meditation as a way to inner wisdom and awareness.

The unconscious wants to work closely with the conscious mind through increasing self-knowledge. The unconscious is also influenced by the quality of conscious thoughts, observations, and experience. I have sometimes wondered if the computer jargon "garbage in, garbage out" applies to this part of the mind, but the mind is wiser than that. It sends danger signals up to a point if it is getting less-than-healthy nourishment, or garbage. If someone refuses to listen to you, the unconscious may become hostile and aggressive, even erupting into violence if all else fails. The mind sends messages of psychic pain, which, like physical pain, tell the sufferer that something needs help and healing. The unconscious wants to be heard as well, and, at times, will even force the issue. For example, recall Sharon from chapter two, whose suppression of one energy pole blocked her creativity and feeling of well-being. By paying heed, you may avoid suffering. As painful as confession, atonement, and other forms of self-knowledge may be, they bring ultimate happiness and well-being to those who practice them.

Fortunately, your unconscious mind prefers to be, like God, gentle, merciful, and loving. God wants you to grow and will show you how if you pay attention to your inner world. This is all the more true if you meditate and work toward behavior that is loving and just. If you ignore your outer experiences and inner sources of wisdom, God may take stronger measures. You may experience more upheaval and chaos, sin, suffering, and crisis until you learn and grow.

Interestingly, mental suffering today brings many people to see psychologists, psychoanalysts, and counselors. These branches of healing emerged only after the Renaissance, Reformation, and Industrial Revolution. As society moved away from a religious base, feasts of atonement and confession became less widespread. Only then did the roles of psychiatrists and psychologists begin to develop. Some say that psychologists are the new confessors; analysts, the new priests. Each discipline, however, does have information to offer. The next section will look at what the psychologists, especially Jung and his followers, have to say about the structures of the unconscious.

JUNG AND THE INNER UNCONSCIOUS

In the course of studying thousands of people both sick and healthy, Jung and his successors discovered a great deal about the inner unconscious life and the powers it exercises, the messages it sends, the polarities it embodies, and the balances it requires. The unconscious has its own needs and rights, and there's trouble when these are neglected. The unconscious needs guidance and enlightenment, but it too can shed its own light. It gives a true assessment of how things are. "The unconscious never lies," said a friend who is a dance and dream therapist. After listening to the dreams of many people, she asserted that wisdom and truth come from this source. As we have seen, your conscious mind, your ego, can shut out what it doesn't want to deal with. The unconscious takes in a great deal more. It is also home to the "Oida" figure that *knows.* You can either misinterpret, suppress, or ignore its messages and take the consequences, or you can take advantage of this storehouse of energy, wisdom, and help. It is your source of hidden manna as you need it.

The Personal Unconscious

Look into this hidden storehouse. Travel first to the level of the pre-conscious or the **personal unconscious.** Here you will find information, impressions, and activities from your experience that were either blocked from your conscious or later dropped by it. From within your inner memory file, you are able to recall material when you need it. Some material, however, is highly charged and difficult for you to handle. These sensitive areas are called **complexes**, systems of energies attached to certain personal associations and experiences like "mother" and "school." Accompanying these complexes are unconscious emotions that have deeply affected you through experience. These complexes unconsciously affect your thoughts, feelings, and actions everyday. For example, many people have problems with authority. This problem stems from childhood, when authority figures literally loomed large. Principals, teachers, and parents were the ones who punished, and they were to be obeyed and sometimes even feared. This anxiety continues into adulthood encounters with authority, resulting in nervousness around priests, police, and others in respectful positions.

A lawyer told me that when accounts of crimes appear in the newspapers, innocent people often come forward to confess, though circumstances prove they couldn't possibly have done it. Their pre-conscious authority complex compels them to do this.

Complexes usually have negative connotations because of the energy they hide. Inferiority complexes are not myths. Too many belittlements and too few affirmations can set a negative energy pattern in someone's head, usually a child's, but adults get them too. In contrast, "associations" are the pleasant, affirming contents of the personal unconscious. They, too, have their hidden energy, but by nature they evoke less attention than complexes.

The Collective Unconscious

On a deeper level of the unconscious is what Jung called the **collective unconscious**, which contains **archetypes** or images that affect all humans everywhere. You need not have personally experienced them; they belong to your collective, inherited, human experience. Usually, however, archetypes are so universal that you inevitably encounter them somewhere—certainly in symbols. Symbols of archetypes differ from culture to culture, but they all proceed from a primordial model or image present in every human, ready to be activated by education and experience. You are affected deeply and powerfully by images of birth, child, mother, death, demon, rebirth, hero, savior, wise old man, God, and so on. The story of the prodigal son affects people so powerfully because we all have inner energies ready to be moved by images of brother, son, father, and forgiveness.

Four key archetypes play a special role in the psyche: the **anima** and the **animus**, and the **persona** and the **shadow**. These come in pairs, with one or the other being favored (as we saw with the personality preferences in chapter five). Many of the same dynamics apply to these unconscious energies.

Masculine and Feminine Archetypes

The anima or the animus is that part of you opposite to your sex. No matter how "macho" a man may be, he has in his unconscious an inner anima or female, while the most feminine of women carries in her unconscious an inner animus or male. Your unconscious opposite helps you relate to the opposite sex externally and helps you gradually achieve a balance of qualities internally. Women as well as men need to be strong and capable of forceful action; men as well as women need to be tender and to nurture life.

The degree and intensity of masculinity and femininity varies in people both externally and internally. Some people can balance these polarities; however, some men are ultra-macho and some women are ultra-feminine. Degrees of difference between the masculine and feminine are not as important as the degree to which one's inner sexual opposite is accepted. Intolerance of the inner animus or anima results in some form of rejection of the opposite sex. This intolerance often leads a person to either withdraw from and quietly reject the opposite sex or noisily conflict and clash with him/her. The outer conflict reflects what is going on inside. The anima or animus can be in conflict if it is not valued and respected enough (consider the woman who nags or puts down her husband, or the man who controls his wife or abuses her). This frequently feeds into external battles. Reconciliation with the inner opposite may help you achieve both inner and outer peace.

Persona and Shadow Archetypes

The persona and the shadow are also opposite archetypes of the unconscious. The word "persona" comes from the use of a mask worn by ancient actors to tell the audience who they were playing. As an archetype, the persona is the part of the psyche that helps you present a favorable front to the rest of the world so that you will be accepted. Some call it the **conformity** archetype; others see it as a civilizing factor that enables people to play a role on the stage of life. For instance, the principal in a school needs to look and act like a principal and exercise the necessary authority to run the school. However, if he wears the persona home—intimidates his wife and children, tries to control them, doesn't relate to them with the warmth and tenderness expected from a husband and father—he displays an imbalanced, inflated persona.

An **inflated persona** causes people to identify continually and in an extreme degree with one of their masks or roles. This state of the mind causes individuals to lose sight of their identity or prevents them from finding their real selves. They become limited and imbalanced. Further, they may become so inflexible in that role that their growth in that persona and in other personas is stifled. Everyone needs a flexible variety of personas appropriate to different areas of life. These personas help people function in various situations while maintaining overall balance.

The persona's opposite is the shadow archetype: the inner child, the creative, vital side that is not easily civilized. It is your source of vitality, creativity, energy, and enthusiasm. It has a strong will and it forcefully advances your actions and ideas. The shadow needs guidance from other areas of the psyche because it can advance terrible ideas and obsessions with the same forcefulness that it advances good ideas. However, while these energies need guidance, they are not meant to be suppressed. If you let the civilized persona overpower your lively shadow, your personality will become flat, dull, lifeless. Worse, the energetic shadow will still make itself felt in tricky ways. If you don't recognize it in yourself, it will project onto other people and distort your outward relationships. Its potential to help you may instead become twisted, like the hag in Sharon's active imagination in chapter two. Its energies, too suppressed for too long, can also erupt into aggression and even violence. Keep it in balance and in harmony, and it will enrich you and help you achieve great goals.

Because the shadow is such a primal part of your being, it may have potentials and qualities you have yet to develop. You may be able to make firm decisions, yet you lack flexibility. Or you may be capable of great fantasies and imaginative stories, but you lack practicality. The shadow side contains much potential for your further growth, your further becoming.

Think of this area of your psyche as the place of your little chaos, your personal *tahawabahu,* the Hebrew word for "the great chaos" described in the beginning of Genesis. From that primal, original chaos the creative hand of God drew the form, the order, the harmony of the earth and all its wonders: the sky, the universe, the cosmos. A little of that chaos remains inside you, waiting to be given form and shape as you develop your potentials and become the best you can be. Together, you and the Creator are forming, bringing into harmony, creating cosmos out of the chaos in your personal world.

The word "education" means "to draw out." The shadow side needs to be educated, to be drawn out, not suppressed. An education overbalanced on the right brain—intellectual, technical, conforming—endangers psychic wholeness and well-being. You also need education in imagination, imagery, symbol, ritual, art, individual expression. You need to recognize and draw into consciousness the gifts and energies of the shadow side. (The process by which this can happen, which Jung terms "individuation," will be described in the next chapter.) Through increased awareness of what is within you (brought about by individuation), you are increasingly able to overcome inner dangers (such as projection), to right imbalances, and to make the greatest creative contribution to life.

To see one example of the shadow's dynamic, try this exercise, which I sometimes give at leadership conferences or workshops on relationships.

1. Take a piece of paper and divide it into three columns. Think of someone you dislike—someone you find difficult to work or socialize with. In the right-hand column list all the qualities you dislike about him/her. In the left- hand column, list all your own strengths all the things you like about yourself.

2. Now try to see if you can find any opposites between what is listed in the left- and right-hand columns. You may discover that the other person's negatives are the exact opposites of your positives. What you really may dislike is not the other person but your own weakness hiding in your inner shadow. You may find that other person to have admirable qualities if you look with unbiased eyes.

Sometimes the shadow is explained by the saying, "If you don't like something in someone else, look for it in yourself." I vividly remember one embarrassing experience of this. I was working at the art center of a community college and, unable to find the tack hammer, went on a rampage looking for it. When it was nowhere to be found, I looked at the sign-out sheet and saw that Virginia had signed it out a week ago. I was furious at her for not returning it right away, according to the rules. I fumed down to where she was working and demanded, "Virginia, where is the tack hammer you signed out last week?" She responded, "Oh, don't you remember? I got it for you when you were hanging the exhibit last week. I don't know what you did with it after that." It was true; I was the guilty party. Virginia had only been a kind and helpful friend.

Only such strong evidence enabled the admittance of my own mistake to override my watchful ego. This was only a minor incident; think how much more on guard against bigger guilts the ego is. Sometimes only a major crisis enables the unconscious energies to break through the barriers and push a person into the conscious choice of growth or regression. With too much repression and too little recognition, the forces that finally break through may be in too much disorder, disarray, and darkness. Instead of growth, violence or psychosis can occur.

But even these calamities will not preclude future growth, as human resources are re-galvanized. One of Jung's patients, a young housewife, had suddenly begun to suffer hallucinations and delusions. Jung spent time with her, entering into her fantasies, accepting them completely as her reality at the time. After this period of being listened to by an accepting person, the woman's delusions suddenly stopped and she returned to normal. After I had read about this, I surmised that the woman had for too long suppressed her shadow. When her shadow energies erupted into illness, she could no longer deny their demands. Although she could not, at that stage, consciously listen to her shadow as it invaded and overrode her conscious mind, another human could be an accepting, listening consciousness for her. Jung enabled her healing by simply accepting those strange images.

DRAWING OUT AND BALANCING OPPOSITE ENERGY POLES

How much better if the shadow side is educated, accepted, formed in a balanced way through inner journeys of meditation, sacrament, art, active imagination, and dreams. How much better if the shadow is gently drawn into consciousness to contribute to growth and to supply its energies to creative works, celebrations, and healthy relationships with others.

Understanding and accepting your inner world helps you to appreciate better your own needs and those of others. Everyone has strengths and weaknesses. If you see the strengths in another person, even though they are different strengths from your own, you are less likely to project on that person the weaknesses of your shadow. If you appreciate your own gifts and needs, if you understand where you are weak and need further development, then you are a long way toward healing and reconciling.

The image of conscious and unconscious energies at opposite poles, at once jostling for attention and expression and balancing each other out, is an exciting one. Opposite poles permeate the whole of creation. There are negative and positive poles in ions, atoms, and in the forces that keep the planets and stars in orbit.

In the previous chapter, I briefly sketched out the following polarities in your consciousness: sensate/intuitive, thinking/feeling, judging/perceiving, and introvert/extrovert. In this chapter I outlined two polarities: anima/animus and persona/shadow. Jung said that life is made up of polarities, and you must try to hold on to both poles. The human tendency, however, is to hold on to one pole and drop the other. This leads to an unbalanced state that can't last very long. If you hold onto one pole, you may swing like a pendulum from one extreme to the other. For example, if your persona energies become too powerful, they may pour out into the shadow. The civilized, highly controlled person you were suddenly erupts like a volcano or does something completely irrational. Such sudden swings create instability. You can sometimes grow and find balance through this process, but the process poses dangers that you can avoid with the wisdom acquired on inner journeys.

You may find balance by preferring one pole enough to make an interesting contribution while learning to appreciate and accept those who contribute in the area of your weakness. For example, Albert Einstein didn't know his own telephone number and was totally inept at many ordinary functions. While he gave the world enormous insights into how things work in the universe, I'd rather trust the corner mechanic with how things work in my car. Einstein may have been overbalanced in one pole, but what a contribution he made! The same may be said for the intuitive poet, the sensory soldier, the analytical scientist, or the emotional actor. Mechanics, musicians, mathematicians, marketing managers, file clerks, farmers, homemakers, house builders, pharmacists, contractors, cooks—all balance each other and contribute to life's harmony.

Communities need these differences not only to survive but to keep life rich and fruitful, interesting and challenging.

The external interaction of many kinds of people finding harmony is analogous to one person's many inner energies seeking recognition and expression. You are an individual work of art in progress. How will all those opposing inner energies find overall balance, resolution, harmony? How can order come out of this chaos? As a painting needs an artist to bring about a lively resolution of all elements, so too does your inner world, your unconscious. This inner artist is sometimes called the **self**. Jung calls it the **transcendent function,** which we will study in the next chapter.

Meditation on a White Stone

PRE-MEDITATION

This meditation will help you and others with whom you share it to focus on one symbol as a means to growth and transformation. The most important part is the dialogue with the Lord into which you will be led. It is also a relaxing way to put aside cares, tensions, and distractions so that your heart and mind, including your deep unconscious, are more prepared for this encounter. If you do it alone, read it slowly onto a cassette tape, then replay it to yourself. Better, have a friend read it to you, then do the same for him or her.

Your body is part of your human wholeness, complete with its wonderful senses and their capacity for gathering impressions from the surrounding world. Your intense observation of things has a spiritual function. As you look at something for what it is (seeing its individual parts and elements), rather than for its practical use, you open up possibilities for growth on all levels, including the spiritual.

This meditation begins with sensory observations, then moves on to the inner senses of memory and imagination. It also observes what Roman Catholics might call a sacramental principle: concrete objects in the visible world at times lead you beyond themselves to an encounter with the invisible God. The concrete object in this meditation is a small, white stone. If possible, have a basket of stones for everyone who participates. If these are not available, skip part one and go directly to part two.

THE MEDITATION

Part One

Find a comfortable, relaxed position as you hold your stone in the palm of your hand. Look at the stone quietly and carefully. Impress on your mind its shape. Look at the colors. Even though it may be almost all white, can you see where the white becomes warmer, or cooler, or lighter, or darker? Close your eyes. What does it feel like? Sense to yourself whether is is soft or hard, large or small, light or heavy, cold or warm, rough or smooth, round or square. Feel it with your fingertips, then with the back of your hand, your arm, perhaps even your cheek.

Open your eyes. Can the stone make any sounds? What happens when it thumps against something soft or hard, such as wood or metal? Does this tell you anything about the stone?

Now put the stone down and relax. Close your eyes again.

Part Two

With your eyes closed, imagine yourself on a beach, the kind where a white pebble or stone may be found. You might remember a seashore you once enjoyed, or envision a photograph or painting of one.

Use your inner senses to picture yourself on the beach by the water. You have wonderful inner senses to help you imagine the sights and sounds.

With your inner sense of hearing, listen to the sounds of the water: the lapping of waves or the crashing of surf. Hear the birds, the sea gulls. Is there a breeze or are there people around? Are there children playing in the distance? Can you hear them?

With your inner sense of smell, catch the special scent of the seashore: the freshness of salt air, suntan oil, perhaps smoke from a nearby campfire.

Use your inner sense of sight to see the wonderful, peaceful colors of the water, sky, and shore. Do you see any grass? Are there dunes, underbrush, cliffs, or trees?

With your inner sense of touch, reach out in your imagination and feel something soft—something you are wearing, your hair, or a piece of seaweed on the beach. Feel the sand beneath you. Perhaps you want to run some of it through your fingers. Perhaps you want to feel the hardness of the pebbles and stones.

Walk down to the water and feel the sudden, cold shock as your feet meet the water; it invigorates your whole body. Now turn toward the shore again to find a warm, pleasant spot on the sand where you will sit down. This is a beautiful, secure spot. You can relax as you feel the warm sun on your head and shoulders.

Smooth, pleasant, white pebbles are all around you. In your imagination, reach out and pick up one that appeals to you. Hold it in your hand and think of all the forces of wind and water that have slowly given it its peaceful shape.

Part Three: A Reflection for Christians

Think of this little pebble or stone as an image of something inside you, a part of you that is faithful like a strong rock, a part of you that is firm and overcomes all obstacles, difficulties, and problems.

Everyday you are being polished, formed by life's events, and problems as well as good times are a part of your formation. But you have an inner strength in Jesus, who is the rock of your salvation, who overcomes the greatest obstacles of sin and death, who shares his victory, his strength, his power to overcome with you.

Jesus made a promise to his followers. He said, "To him who overcomes, I will give a white pebble on which is written a new name."

Part Four: A Reflection for Everyone

Think of the pebble you are holding in your imagination's hand as a symbol of the wonderful, faithful you that is growing, polished every day by life's events under the loving care of God. You are finding your deepest, truest, most beautiful self as you overcome in God, as you are faithful, as you live and grow in God's Life.

As you hold the pebble, sitting on your inner beach, thank the Lord for the beautiful, wonderful "you" he is forming every day. Thank the Lord for being your strength, for helping you to overcome difficulties and obstacles, for giving you a new identity, strong and whole.

Take time to listen to the Lord for a few minutes. Listen to what he tells you about the new "you" he is forming, about the new gifts he wants to develop in you. Listen to God tell you about how he wants to be your strong helper at all times.

Now see a beautiful mosaic spreading out in your mind's eye, forming itself before you, filled with stones of many brilliant glowing colors, jewel-like, reflecting the sun. See the stone you're holding become a shining white or a glowing color and find a place in the mosaic that needs it, a place your stone will enrich. Place your stone there.

Thank the Lord for making you a part of his great mosaic of life. Listen to him tell you where he wants you to shine, and thank him again. Talk to the Lord and listen a bit longer. When you are finished, open your eyes.

POST-MEDITATION

If you keep a journal, here are some questions to answer in it. If you do this meditation with a group of people, use these question to stimulate discussion or further activity.

1. How did you feel before the meditation? During the meditation? How do you feel now? Did you see or hear anything interesting? What was your shore

scene like? What kind of mosaic did you see? Was it a picture or an abstract design? Did your stone become a color? Where did you see a need for it?

2. Did you receive any messages from the Lord? Were they new, or reinforcement of things you already knew? Did they confirm any previous feelings or hunches?

If you are writing in a journal, write down anything you learned during this time. In a group, provide an opportunity to share while respecting privacy. You can say, "Would you like to share any inner messages about gifts that want to develop in you now, or do you want to keep it a secret between you and God?" If you do this meditation with children, provide art supplies and say, "Can you give us just a little hint in a drawing?" or "Would you like to draw you or your stone?" Provide other options for drawing: the shore scene or the mosaic.

Art is a good post-meditation experience for people of all ages. Provide for yourself or the group cutout squares of color from magazines and construction paper, or make small squares of felt. Ask, "Would anyone like to make a mosaic? Remember that God wants to form something beautiful, like a mosaic, out of all our lives as we love one another and work in harmony together."

The image of a white stone is a reminder that God is forming a part of you, the inner, hidden part you can't see, to be forever unique and beloved in God's sight. The image of a mosaic reminds you that God forms something beautiful in your life as you grow together with others.

7. Journey to Your Higher Self

A HUMAN, INNER ECOSYSTEM

The science of ecology has uncovered the importance of interrelationships in nature. This is a complex and fragile world where many parts balance out to make a whole. If one part of the ecosystem becomes unbalanced, a whole species can be destroyed. When a species is destroyed, the whole ecology may suffer. Experts are beginning to see the importance of both the whole and the parts that make up that whole. Balance is key.

In humans, there is an ecology with a psychological ecosystem. The last few chapters considered some of the opposing energies in your inner world. How do all these come into balance, harmony, and wholeness? These are life-giving goals of inner journeys, fruits of the renewing inner encounter with God.

John Sanford hears a call to wholeness in the words of Jesus, "Be perfect, as your Father in heaven is perfect." Sanford's translation reads, "Be ye whole, as your Father in heaven is whole."[1] This, in fact, is the goal of the human life journey. God, the Creator, created order, harmony, and life out of the *tahawabahu,* the primal chaos described in the beginning of Genesis. The Creator and the results of this creative action are the very opposite of chaos, disorder, disintegration, and death. God is the I AM who revealed his identity to Moses in the burning bush, where fire illuminated but did not destroy life. You also are called to be illuminated and transformed by God as you encounter the holy presence in your own life. I AM calls you to continually become in wholeness and harmony and to overcome the entropy that destroys.

God embraces the whole of creation in fullness. You are made in God's image, thus there must be, within your limited scope, a potential for balance and wholeness. The many tensions, forces, energies, and opposites in you can also come into balance and fullness. You can become within yourself a well-designed work of art, an ordered cosmos.

THE ARTIST AS COSMOS BUILDER

The arts provide good examples of small wholes in the context of the great cosmic whole—small harmonies resolving opposites in the context of the cosmic harmony. This is one reason why people find satisfaction in a great painting, symphony, drama, or story. There is craft to each art, and artists must master the basic techniques and structures. A really great work of art is put together the way the great cosmos is put together: with rhythm, balance, tension, resolution, areas of intensity, and peace. For example, Cezanne's landscapes reflect not only the superficial appearances of the earth but also some of its underlying structures.

The play *Sunday in the Park with George* is the onstage re-creation of the pointillist painting, *Sunday Afternoon on the Island of Grande Jette.* The nineteenth-century artist George Seurat painstakingly created this scene with thousands of tiny dots of color.

In the play, people depicted in the painting come to life. Their nineteenth-century gowns, bustles, bonnets, uniforms, and suits separate from the green park backdrop and symbolize playfulness, love, loyalty, jealousy, deceit, rivalry, and hate. The human passions that heave beneath the calm Sunday scene gradually build up to a climactic cacophony of confusion. At the height of the chaos, an actor playing Seurat stands slightly outside the scene to cry out, "Order! Design! Tension! Balance! Harmony!" As he does so, the figures quiet down and arrange themselves into the ordered cosmos of the painting.

One lesson to be learned from this wonderful play is that—difficult as they are to achieve in the arts—order, tension, balance, harmony, and wholeness are even harder to achieve in humans. Artists who have learned their craft can do it with a painting. Fortunately, you have within yourself an inner artist, a higher Self, capable of bringing you into your own order, harmony, and wholeness. One of the most important goals of an inner journey is to touch this inner artist, to allow this creative inner presence its transformational scope.

THE INNER ARTIST AND INDIVIDUATION

When, in chapter five, you explored the conscious mind with its own opposite energies, you learned how the ego functioned as a gatekeeper and something of an organizer. Psychologists describe a self existing at an even deeper level with a more profound organizing function. Some psychologists describe it as an archetype, albeit the most powerful and profound of all the unconscious energies. Others describe it as far more. Though it emerges from the same deep areas of the collective unconscious, the self ideally encompasses both the unconscious and conscious mind. Its function is described as bringing about **individuation**. Through individuation, energies in the unconscious are gradually drawn into consciousness and balance. The process enables you to become whole, transformed, holy, your truest self.

The process of individuation opposes the process of entropy in your psychological life. **Entropy** is the process by which things run down, disintegrate, die, or, by dictionary definition, "the doctrine of inevitable social decline and degeneration" (*The Random House*

Dictionary of the English Language, second ed.,
unabridged, def. 4). Conversely, through individuation,
life can be healed, renewed, transformed, brought into
balance, made whole. While God is the life-giving power
that generates renewal, the self is the orchestrator of the
action in you.

THE INNER CHRIST, THE UNIFIER

Some psychologists refer to this inner orchestrator as
the Self (capital S) or the Higher Self to differentiate it
from the ordinary self. Psychologists with a spiritual
orientation even refer to the Self as "the Christ principle
within," and Jung accepted this terminology. This leads
to some interesting word associations. The word "devil"
stems from the Greek word *diabolos*, with meanings
ranging from "throwing a javelin" to "tearing apart." It
evokes a sense of opposition and destruction to life,
wholeness, and harmony.

The word "religion" stems from the Greek words "re"
("again") and "ligio" ("to tie together"). Think of
ligaments, the cords that tie together muscles and bones
and enable most people to be physically active. Think
also of the many uses of "re," such as "redo" ("to do over
again"). Religion, in its earliest word derivation, means
to bind back or to bind together again, the very opposite
of "tearing apart" or *diabolos*.

Although history has shown religion to be, at times,
painfully divisive, many of the great leaders and
founders originally sought and taught unity. Eastern
religions speak of "The many in one." Jesus prayed "that
they all may be one, as Thou, Father in me, and I in
Thee, that they may be one in us." One of his credentials
as one sent from God was the power to heal and to cast
out demons, the *diabolos* spirit that tears people apart.
He also left information so that true followers could be
recognized: "Peace I leave with you," and "By this will

all know that you are my disciples, that you have love for one another." These credentials are similar to the goals of the Higher Self in you.

A good look at the energies of inner chaos and cosmos will uncover evidence that the individuating archetype of the Self and the inner Christ are either closely linked or one and the same. Some psychologists have actively worked with the Higher Self in their patients to bring about healing and individuation. On that level, an organizing archetype reflects and possibly touches the Christ as a master pattern for unity within you. Perhaps that is why Jesus said, "The kingdom of God is within you."

THE INNER ANGEL AND INDIVIDUATION

The "Oida" angel in Revelation sheds further light on the inner- unifying principle. While his messages are originally addressed to the Churches, they are also for each member of the Churches, since one who acknowledges the presence of God in him/herself is, in effect, a little temple of the Lord. The great message to the larger community is also meant for individuals; in both cases, this unifying message relates to the situations at hand. The "Oida" angel is your personal guide, and he speaks to you for God if you are ready to listen.

As the "Oida" angel appeared to John at a time of persecution and crisis for John's community, so does inner guidance often come forward in times of personal crisis. At these times you are forced to be more attentive to what is going on around you, and your defending ego is often overwhelmed. Your past defenses and parameters dissolve, and your awareness is forced to expand. More of the unconscious content is suddenly drawn into consciousness by individuation. In John's crisis his awareness expands to include an angel. You may also look for some angelic harmony and growth when you are faced with a crisis.

To make the best of such a time, however, you need to be in tune with your inner sources of life. Revelation reveals that John's angel appeared to a man of many inner journeys, a man already attuned to inner wisdom and ready to receive further knowledge. To be ready to listen to your own inner angel, even in times of crisis, it is wise to learn to journey inward and prepare beforehand.

The contents of the angel's message to John's historic community are interesting. In his encouragements and warnings, the angel makes it clear that the greatest dangers are not from the outside, in spite of all the persecutions that are taking place at the time. It is the dissension, mediocrity, vanity, and compromise with evil within the communities that provoke the warnings.[2] Today, too, the outer difficulties in life don't bring you the greatest danger; rather, what happens within as you go through good and bad times either does you in or brings you to fulfillment. The times of crisis force you to turn to God and the Higher Self.

Another image in Revelation points to unity with God as the way to realize your most whole and high Self. The "Oida" angel begins each message with the words "I know" and ends with a great promise: "To the one who overcomes, I will give a white pebble on which is written a new name, to be know only be the one who receives it."

THE WHITE PEBBLE OR PROMISE

Stone is the symbol of something that endures. It signifies that part of you that will endure. In dream imagery, Jung found that a stone appeared to people in dreams just when they were on the point of individuation, self-discovery, getting it all together. One man dreamed of two lions polishing a large, beautiful, round stone. Jung saw in this an image of the man's true self being polished, formed by the events of his life.[3]

In both dream and scripture, the stone's roundness speaks of the wholeness and integrity brought about by individuation. Its symbolism of the Self is reinforced by the person's receiving a new name written on the stone, which signifies the transformation brought about by individuation.

The stone is also a symbol of protection. In the time when Revelation was written, it was a pagan custom to wear an amulet, a stone or other object worn around the neck for protection from evil.[4] A name that no one else was allowed to know was on the amulet. If someone else knew the name inside the amulet, then he had power over the person wearing it. The angel's promise of a white stone with a secret name meant not only individuation and transformation in God but also protection from evil.

The context of this image in Revelation is also pertinent. The visions present an invisible reality underlying the visible world. A great struggle is going on between good and evil—between chaos and the harmony, life, and love of God. The vision says, in word and symbol, that no one has to be alone in this struggle. The *diabolos*—the tearing apart, destructive, death elements—can be overcome in the world and in the individual psyche.

The great message of Revelation is that God is greater than chaos and evil and has already won the definitive battle against them. Life, love, cosmos will prevail. The good news is that you also can share in the victory and the promises. The Lord, who heals bodies, minds, and spirits, says, "To him (her) who overcomes I will give a white pebble, with a new name written on it." The new name symbolizes the highest individuation and transformation through which you become your true self—at one within, at one with others, and at one with God.

Forest Meditation

PRE-MEDITATION

As you begin this meditation, place yourself in the presence of the Creator, in whatever name, word, or image best expresses for you this mysterious, transcendent dimension of existence. For some it might be simply "God"; for others it may be "Lord," "Jesus," "Holy Spirit," "Great Father," "Great Spirit," "Good Shepherd," or any other names that help people experience the Nameless. Ask for openings and insights as you make this meditation journey. Allow the dialogue to continue at any point it occurs. You can return later to take up the path of this meditation. Its purpose will be fulfilled more directly when your own dialogue with the Transcendent happens.

THE MEDITATION

The Forest

Relax, breathe deeply, and close your eyes. Sink further and further into relaxation as you see yourself walking through a cool and shady forest path. See the trees high overhead, the ferns and forest plants beneath as you go along.

You come to a little clearing in the forest, where a strong shaft of light beams down onto a plant that looks like a rosebush. Hanging on the bush is a sign that says, "Water me." You look around the clearing, and you see at the edge a watering can full of water. You carry it over to the bush and pour the water all around it: the roots, the leaves, the top. Replace the watering can, and when you turn back to the plant you see a rosebud forming at the very top. You return to the plant to see another sign beneath the rosebud that says, "This is for you," and you see your name. You pick the rosebud on its stalk and continue on the path that leads back into the forest.

You enter the shady forest again and the path grows steadily darker as it works through more tangle and growth. You come to another little clearing, not as bright as the last one, and you see a knapsack on the path that looks vaguely familiar. You examine it, and it looks exactly like a problem—a tangle—you are coping with in life. What is the problem? Do you need to look inside the knapsack to find out more about it? Open the knapsack, and let more of the problem reveal itself.

Now close the knapsack and put it on your back to take with you. The rose is in your hand as you continue through the dark forest tangle.

When the forest seems darkest, when you can see no more than a few feet ahead, you see a large, dark wall in front of you. It is made of stone and covered over with ivy and moss. You want to go beyond the wall, so you begin to push the ivy aside as you walk along the wall to see if there is an opening. You walk, peering through ivy until you see a dark, old, wooden door, made of heavy oak with iron hinges and an ancient lock. You push against the door with all your might, but it will not budge. You think of all the things in your life right now that will not seem to budge, and you wonder how you can move them aside to go forward.

Then something rustles behind you, and a gentle voice says, "Do you need a key?" You turn around to see an ancient woman with a wise and friendly face. She holds in front of her a wooden box as ancient as the door you want to open. You ask her if she has a key for you. She answers, "Yes, indeed I do. What do you have for me?" She is looking at the rose in your hand, so you give it to her. She holds out the box. You open it and inside lies a golden key. It resembles one of the keys you are looking for in your life right now. What shape does it take? Examine the key to see what is has to say to you.

The Garden

Now, with the key in your hand, the door opens by itself and closes as you walk into a garden filled with light. As you enter the garden, you see roses and many other flowers, all your favorites, tumbling over each other in a merry confusion of color. One of the paths leads to the center. You follow this path and in the center you see a fountain.

You sit by the fountain and listen to the bubbling water, smell the flowers, hear birdsong, and enjoy the feeling of abundant life you have discovered in this secret place. You feel comforted by the warm sun shining down on you. As you relax, you begin to sense a presence, warm and loving, that is somehow vaguely familiar to you. You relax even further into this loving presence and you know it wants to talk with you about the problem in your knapsack.

Tell this loving presence about the problem. Share all your feelings. Let out any hurts, frustration, angers, and fears you feel. Face the problem and your feelings squarely. Let your feelings find expression with this accepting presence that you somehow know.

Feel the comfort of the acceptance and love around you as you clear your heart. Begin to sense that you are to take off the knapsack. You remove it from your shoulders, but instead of falling to the ground, the knapsack rises like a balloon, taking you along with it. You and the knapsack rise higher and higher into the sunlight, into the loving presence, to where you have a star's-eye view of your life. You look down on your life from afar and focus on the problem. From this higher viewpoint, you see the pulls and tensions, the people, the situation. Now you have a better view of how others feel, of what their hurts and needs are. You have a better view of what needs to be changed around you or within you. You see how to right this situation, how to accept it, how to make it work for you and others.

The Roses

The loving presence is very strong now, showing you more about this situation and about your life. Look and listen peacefully. Relish the light and insight from your star's-eye view. Let go of the knapsack. See it float away into the light as you float back to the garden. Now there are even more roses than before. You pick them along with other flowers. You walk back toward the oak door and it opens for you by itself.

As you return through the forest, you meet people you love and care about, and you give them roses. See their faces light up as they receive their gifts. Notice how your arms stay full of flowers no matter how many you give away. You all return to the forest's edge—back to your waking life—in a celebration walk, exchanging flowers and love.

It will soon be time to leave your inner forest with its secret garden. Know that you can always return here, in meditation, to touch your inner place of life. Know that you will have more roses of peace and love to share with others. Prepare now to take these roses with you as you return to your waking life, and open your eyes.

8. *Journey Toward Cosmos*

WATER AS AN INNER STORM IMAGE

Two of my favorite Bible stories involve a large body of water, the sea of Galilee, in a stormy state. In one story, Jesus takes his disciples out on a boat to where the crowds can no longer reach them. Jesus is exhausted after his work of meeting the need and demands of others. He relaxes and falls asleep. I picture the disciples also finding a few moments of peace and quiet.

Not for long. A storm arises, and the little boat, tossed by wind and waves, seems in danger. Jesus sleeps on, but the disciples are terrified. They wake up the master. Jesus stretches his arms out over the water and calms the storm, stills the waves.

In the other story, the disciples are again in a boat, but this time Jesus has remained ashore. However, in the night, he comes to them walking on water. The enthusiastic Peter wants to join Jesus immediately, and Jesus invites him to do so. He begins to walk on the water, and does well as long as he looks at Jesus. However, when he looks at the rough waters, fear overcomes Peter and he begins to sink. Jesus rescues Peter and brings him safely to the boat.

These stories have often inspired people to trust in God when things get tough. The Lord will calm your inner turmoil and help you solve your dilemmas. If you keep your eyes on God, and not on the overwhelming problem, you won't sink beneath them. I remember singing the following song (one of my favorites) in a Lutheran young people's choir in Brooklyn:

Though the angry surges roll
O'er my tempest driven soul,
I am peaceful, for I know,
Wildly though the winds may blow,
I've an anchor safe and sure,
That will ever more endure.
And it holds, my anchor holds,
My anchor holds.

The anchor was Jesus, and my inner storms were the overwhelming vicissitudes of adolescent crisis: looks, clothes, social invitations, grades, popularity, boys, acceptance. Though I knew little of theology, psychology, and literature at the time, water aptly symbolized my inner turmoils.

Later I discovered that, in literature, water often symbolizes the unconscious; in theology, water at once symbolizes death and life, chaos and creation, sin and deliverance.

In scripture, the image of water begins with the first chapter of Genesis and goes all the way through to the last book, Revelation or Apocalypse. The image of water carries much of the mystery of the call to work with God in creating cosmos out of chaos, harmony out of complexity, new life out of entropy. It was appropriate that Jesus called Peter to join him on the stormy waters. People are often called to calm storms, and they either go forward, buoyed up by the powers of their inner, unconscious energies, or else they sink beneath them. Inner energies can be friend or foe.

Happily, deep within you exists the inner artist, the Christ, the Higher Self, which was discussed in the preceding chapters. This great friend is ready to show you how to find—despite the opposing poles of your inner unconscious energies—a support rather than a morass, a help rather than a hindrance. As you befriend this unifying power and give yourself over to its process (akin to individuation), you begin to overcome evil, confusion, chaos. You find a role in the creation of unity, harmony, life, cosmos.

ORIGINAL AND SECONDARY CHAOS

Your role in such creation is that of a little partner with the Great Creator in whose image you are created. As you open the Bible as it now stands, the first image you will find is that of God drawing a harmonious cosmos out of chaotic waters. Read Genesis 1:1.[1] In the beginning there was the *tahawabahu*—the waste, the void, the chaos—out of which the Spirit of God, brooding over the dark waters, brought light, land, creatures, the ordered world we love. The word itself, *tahawabahu,* sounds some of the primal confusion. The image of the dark waters calls to mind the surging ocean with its mighty, uncontrollable, mysterious forces.

A certain amount of chaos, or *tahawabahu,* or unformed possibilities still remain in creation. Perhaps this is so that people can work with God to bring about fullness and completion. After all, people—you—are made in the image of the Creator. You, along with everyone else, are a co-creator, able to bring order out of chaos, to generate new life and new possibilities. "Be fruitful and multiply" are the words of God to humans in the creation poem.

A little bit of the *tahawabahu* also remains inside people: in their unformed possibilities, in their polarized inner energies, in their sea of emotions, which also include the effects of sin. You are again invited to be in creative partnership with God in bringing about a fullness, a wholeness, that realizes your maximum potential.

Some scripture scholars and theologians make an interesting connection between cosmos, chaos, and sin. Monika Hellwig, an eminent Roman Catholic theologian, addresses chaos and sin in a talk on Baptism.[2] Hellwig pictures the mighty hand, the Word, the Wisdom of God, drawing an ordered cosmos out of the chaos. This image includes the roiling waters of the primeval *tahawabahu*.

In the Noah story, the water image appears again as the result of sin. Hellwig cannot see a spiteful God destroying the creation and creatures that He formed with such tender care, because further revelation has shown us a God of compassion and love.

To solve this dilemma, Hellwig and other theologians ask if there might not be something built into the way things are made that automatically reverts to a secondary chaos, related to the original *tahawabahu*, that kicks in when the ordering principles are too outrageously flouted.

If humans, who were created to live in loving, just, and compassionate relationships, turn on one another—if they manipulate, enslave, and exploit each other—they throw up blocks that close off God's creative, loving, ordering flow. When this happens, not only will society become chaotic, but a greater chaos, such as the flood, may be automatically released. The destroying waters may be a secondary chaos, the result of sin, reverting back to the primeval chaos that existed before the creation of cosmic order.

In his book *Original Blessing,* Matthew Fox cites several people who foreshadowed this view.[3] Medieval mystic Hildegarde of Bingen saw the cosmos itself, not God, keeping a ledger, because the cosmos will not in the long run stand for disruption of its harmonies. Paul Ricoeur saw Cosmos and Psyche as two poles—outer and inner—of the same expressive power. Chinese philosophy also saw the same rules for microcosms and macrocosms—they are to each other "like inner and outer world." St. Paul wrote of a relationship between Christian and creation in Romans 8:22,23:

> Yes, we know that all creation groans and is in agony even until now. Not only that, but we ourselves, although we have the Spirit as first fruits, groan inwardly while we await the redemption of our bodies.

Hellwig again applies this theme in Exodus, where water again plays a part. As the Jews flee from Pharaoh's soldiers, the Red, or Reed, Sea permits them to pass in safety. (They are, after all, trusting Yahweh's leadership on their way to founding a community based on the justice of the Torah and Law.) The Egyptians, bent on enslaving and exploiting their fellow humans, suffer the death-dealing, destructive powers of the water. Nature helps those working toward harmonious relations with God and fellow humans; those bent on cruelty, exploitation, and greed find a nature reverted to chaos.

Hellwig relates these biblical events to the water used in Baptism and the new order of life according to the Spirit water symbolizes. Many people baptized today are babies, with the choice being made by the parents. A crucial question is whether the parents, and later the child, make further choices to live out what the water symbolizes. Are the parents and children, like the ancient Israelites, journeying toward more harmonious and ethical ways of relating to their fellow humans? Are they making inner journeys that put them in touch with the life-giving Spirit that lives within?

COSMOS-BUILDING CHOICES

You also have, within your limitations and circumstances, many choices to make, including what attitude you take toward external experiences. You also have the power of choice over portions of your inner life. If you choose, you can move, by at least an iota, toward freedom. You can direct your inner energies toward growth, integration, harmony, generativeness, and life. You can also choose further inertia, dissolution, disharmony, sin, and chaos.

You may not, at present, have the capacity to become a mighty cosmos builder with great inner energies that support life. However, you do have, at any given moment, the capacity to choose to move in that direction.

Deuteronomy 30:15 speaks the words of God: "I have set before you life and prosperity, death and doom..." and in verse 19,

> I call heaven and earth to witness...I have set before you life and death, the blessing and the curse. Choose life then, that you and your descendants may live, by loving the Lord your God, heeding his voice, and holding fast to him.[4]

Your capacity to become a cosmos builder depends upon many small choices; the more choices you make toward life, the more your direction toward life is confirmed and reinforced. Gradually, your inner energies, even the unconscious ones, work toward wholeness and balance until they support you, as the water responds to Jesus' wishes and supports him. The God-life in your depths, your Higher Self, wishes to bring your personal world into harmony so that you become increasingly creative and life-giving, skilled in creating cosmos.

A CHAOS-TO-COSMOS STORY

I found myself invited to make one such small choice, the kind that comes up often and prepares us for bigger choices. I was walking along in anger during an office lunch hour, with my little inner voice going full force: "That was so insulting. If she didn't like the idea, why didn't she tell me while we were planning, instead of coming out with all this negativity in front of an already-complaining observer. It was so unprofessional, so unjust, so demeaning—". And then I caught myself.

Shortly before, a co-worker, Janet, had enthusiastically joined a visitor, Helen, with complaints about strategies aimed at helping our struggling youth program. We were in the period between when something starts and when it begins to run smoothly. People were swift with complaints before results could even be seen. Earlier, Helen and others had complained about a situation that this new venture would solve, given time. I thought our efforts deserved more time and patience. I also felt sensitive about the whole thing, even more so because solving the problem was also overworking both my co-worker and myself.

Janet's outburst got to me. I saw a need to separate her from Helen, to keep the negatives from ganging up on me. But as I maneuvered Helen to another room, I saw an exchange of glances between her and Janet. Their knowing smiles spoke of complicity. During the rest of the conversation, I found myself dealing with defensive feelings as well as a difficult visitor who continued to find fault with everything, including details out of my jurisdiction. I realized it was gripe time; my efforts to be open and non-judging were being strained, and I graciously ended the interview. By this time, however, I was not feeling at all gracious. My inner world was in turmoil, so I walked. That's when I took note of my inner situation.

A voice inside was issuing a steady stream of anger and accusation toward Helen, Janet, young people of a certain age, their parents, even myself. I had, after all, been dumb enough to take on the burdens of change. This voice addressed the whole situation in which I found myself: cramped working quarters, necessary overtime, lack of appreciation. Worse, I had to do so much because others weren't handling their functions well. They took it easy without considering any consequences, while I saw needs and overworked myself. It was unfair, right?

As my inner chaos hit a crescendo, I suddenly realized I was heading in a miserable direction: further and further into frustration, conflict, and unhappiness. And I was doing nothing to solve the problem.

I decided then and there not to let conflict and chaos have the last word. I took myself in hand. "I don't have time to listen to this," I told myself. "I'm not a robot. I'm a human being, and I have a choice. Right now I can choose conflict or peace, misery or happiness, chaos or cosmos. The conflict and chaos isn't getting me anywhere, so I'll choose peace. It's a great day out. I like walking and looking at the autumn leaves. Problems can be solved. I won't let the chaos prevail."

Within a few minutes, I was at peace. I ultimately saw the beautiful qualities, the care and concern in Janet, Helen, and others involved. I recognized more of the factors that caused the unrest in all of us. Some concrete, practical solutions slowly filtered into my consciousness. I felt better as my energies began to find creative, constructive directions again. I was turning from a victim of chaos into a co-creator of cosmos.

REVELATIONS OF COSMOS CONSCIOUSNESS

It was then that a passage from scripture came to mind that had puzzled me. The last book of the Bible has some strong images of water. In Revelation, clear, sparkling rivers of life flow out from the throne of the lamb and from the ordered cosmos of the New Jerusalem, the City of God.[5] Water is clearly an expression of a New Creation with its abundance of life, justice, harmony, and order. In another passage, however, the water images are more confusing.

In Revelation 12, a great sign appears in the sky: a woman in labor. A dragon, the devil, waits to swallow up the child as it is born, but the child is snatched up to heaven and safety. The woman is given the wings of an eagle to fly to the desert and safety. The frustrated dragon sends out a torrent of water from his mouth to try and sweep her away. The friendly earth comes to her rescue and swallows up the water. The enraged dragon then goes off to wage war on the rest of the woman's offspring, taking up a position by the shore of the sea.

These images are the stuff of dreams, the kind of messages the unconscious sends to tell about the true state of affairs. After reading this passage, I had thought, "There must be some good psychology embedded in this passage." The waters of the ocean so often signify the creative unconscious—those mysterious, inner parts brimming with rich possibilities waiting to be formed, made conscious, brought into the light. If this is so, would not the earth represent the conscious mind, that part of the inner geography that you know in a more direct way? Conscious consideration of a situation will often swallow up a stream of unconscious chaos when it threatens your psyche. Individuation is based on the process of unconscious energies becoming conscious.

THE DRAGON: YOUR FIRST THOUGHT

What about that image of the dragon waiting on the beach? That still puzzled me. I thought of this while my chaotic and angry thoughts about my secretary, my critics, and the human race began to turn around.

The seashore seems to represent that first line of awareness, that beachhead where impressions from the outer world and energies from the inner world sometimes lap up on, sometimes storm onto, the conscious mind. When I can control these first-resulting thoughts, I can control a great deal: my feelings, my reactions, my present state of happiness and productivity.

On the occasion of the anger described above, I realized that this little voice was on the narrow, first border of consciousness, angry and accusing toward all. The beast symbolizes Satan, who is called "the accuser," the one ready to point out the worst in everything that happens and in everyone involved. In the image of the beast, he stations himself, allegorically, on the shore, the dividing line between conscious and unconscious, ready to influence what enters your awareness and that first critical thought in response. The vulnerable ego easily admits what is negative about others; you become defensive, hostile; a great deal of chaos ensues. You get into a real stew, as I did, with vital energies dissipated and nothing constructive accomplished.

At these times, you feel like a victim of circumstances, and inner chaos takes over. However, another inner energy is available to help you to overcome, to make a choice, to choose life, peace, harmony, and constructive action over negativity and confusion. Sometimes it's a fine line, a delicate inner nuance that permits you to choose your thoughts and reactions and to overcome rather than succumb. Sometimes you have to insist, to shout to yourself, "Peace! Peace! Peace!" Gentle or forceful, the inner energy that helps you make this crucial choice is one that is strengthened by inner journeys to your hidden wisdom.

YOUR POWER TO CHOOSE

Most often, the little choices and decisions help you train yourself for the big ones. They help you hone your capacity for making good choices; they will help you win your inner battle. But it's contact with the living presence of God's Spirit that enables you to see, discern, and know what the wise choice is in each situation. The great message of hope throughout scripture comes through loud and clear: In God, you can do it; you can overcome; you can choose cosmos instead of succumbing to chaos.

As you overcome, you are promised the morning star of new beginnings, the hidden manna of total nourishment, the white pebble with a new name that brings an identity that will endure. You are promised the crown and scepter of king- or queenship, to rule your cosmos rather than be rules by chaos. You are promised that the tears of your struggles will be wiped away by the hand of your Creator. You will dwell in a new creation, a city of exquisite order, harmony, beauty, and light that is continuously refreshed by sparkling waters of life. Your unconscious and conscious energies will find balance; your will interact with others in harmonies of affirmation and joy. Both the inner and outer cosmos will shine.

As you now make your choices—both little and big ones—keep your vision high and clear and renew it often with inner journeys. Your struggles with confusion and chaos, along with your efforts to create cosmos, love, and life, will bring you closer to realizing the wonderful promises, with foretastes of their joys along the way. It's worth the work.

Chaos-to-Cosmos Meditation: The City

PRE-MEDITATION

The first chapter of the Bible pictures the Hebrew Ruah, the breath or spirit of God, blowing over the chaos. The following meditation will help you expand this image and then apply it to your contemporary life.

THE MEDITATION

Picture an angry, dark, turbulent ocean in a storm; it's a chaotic scene: dark, swirling, angry waters tear apart everything in their path. This is the primal chaos that the ancient Hebrews called *tahawabahu*.

Ask your inner artist, your imagination, to create for you a symbol of the great creative power of God; it might be a dove, a mighty hand stretched out, or the creative breath of God, the Ruah, hovering over the waters. Picture the creative power of God hovering over the *tahawabahu*, the dark chaos; drawing forth light, sun, stars, planets; forming the universe, the harmonious, ordered cosmos, our beautiful planet earth. Visualize things on earth that you love: mountains, plains, trees, plants, flowers, butterflies, birds, and animals.

Look at just one of the parts of creation, a single tree, and see a rhythm, a unifying structure running through all the branches from the largest limb down to the tiniest twig. Look at other kinds of trees—a pine, oak, weeping willow, or palm—to see how different they are. So there is rich variety as well as unity in creation.

Say "thank you" to God for the richness and variety that run through creation, and for the unity, the harmony, the beauty that pervade it.

Think of some ways humans use these natural resources: trees made into houses, stone made into cities and works of art...

Imagine a beautiful city where all the buildings and streets are planned in perfect order and enriched with trees, plants, statues, and fountains. This city is like a visual symphony with a wonderful harmony. See a band of musicians stroll through the streets, filling the city with lively music.

Now picture this city filled with people building new structures, working to keep it clean and orderly, caring for the needs of others, providing food, clothing, housing, healing, and education. Picture some people creating music and art that reflect the beauty and order of the universe.

Realize that God has called you to work as a partner in creation, as a co-creator, to maintain and further the great work of cosmos building. Say "thank you" to God for creating you in God's own image: a creative, life-giving person. Realize that you are empowered by the breath of the Holy Spirit to further the creation process, the cosmos making, in partnership with God. Thank God for calling you to create cosmos.

This call to be a co-creator does not only apply to the material world—building houses, cities, systems—but also to your interaction with others. Thank God for calling you to work as a partner according to your gifts in caring for his people on earth.

Ask the Creator to show you some of your gifts, given so you can work for a better, more beautiful and just world. Let God tell you how you are to be a creative cosmos builder working for the good of all.

Thank God for calling you to be a partner in this great creative work, for calling you to be a cosmos builder. Thank God. Listen again, and when you feel ready, open your eyes.

POST-MEDITATION

Are there any blocks in yourself, others, society, environment, or the world that hinder you and others from giving and working to build cosmos? Some elements of those dark, angry, destructive waters—that *tahawabahu*, that chaos—always seem to get in the way of harmony. People get lazy, think only of themselves, and make demands. Ask God to help you see and overcomes obstacles to your own work with Him in creating cosmos, beauty, harmony, a well-ordered creation.

Write out a list of obstacles and work them into a prayer that asks God's help in overcoming these obstacles.

Divide a paper into halves. On one side draw the obstacles: on the other, draw how they are overcome. Draw pictures that came to you in the meditation. Explain to the group or one-on-one with a friend what you saw and felt.

Make a list of talents you can use to create cosmos, a more beautiful, harmonious, loving world.

Chaos-to-Cosmos Meditation: The House

PRE-MEDITATION

You may prefer to use this warmer, closer meditation, especially with young people. I've done this with students as young as eighth graders. I ask them to prepare to use their imaginations, their inner artists, to meditate on their own roles in building cosmos in partnership with the Creator. I instruct them to relax, settle down, and close their eyes so they can call upon their inner artist.

The introduction and discussion in the city meditation also apply to this one.

THE MEDITATION

Picture an angry, dark, turbulent ocean in a storm; it's a chaotic scene: dark, swirling, angry waters tear apart everything in their path. This is the primal chaos that the ancient Hebrews called *tahawabahu*.

Ask your inner artist, your imagination, to create for you a symbol of the great creative power of God; it might be a dove, a mighty hand stretched out, or the creative breath of God, the Ruah, hovering over the waters. Picture the creative power of God hovering over the the *tahawabahu*, the dark chaos; drawing forth light, sun, stars, planets; forming the universe, the harmonious, ordered cosmos, our beautiful planet earth. Visualize things on earth that you love: mountains, plains, trees, plants, flowers, butterflies, birds, and animals.

Look at just one of the parts of creation, a single tree, and see a rhythm, a unifying structure running through all the branches, from the largest limb down to the tiniest twig. Look at other kinds of trees—a pine, oak, weeping willow, or palm—to see how different they are. So there is rich variety as well as unity in creation.

Say "thank you" to God for the richness and variety that run through creation. Say "thank you" for the unity, the harmony, and the beauty that pervade it.

Focus on trees again. See a man with a wagonload of lumber come down a road through the forest. He comes to his house, where neighbors are working to put on finishing touches. With strong arms he carries the wood to where his neighbors can use it.

What is this house like? Can you see grass, flowers, and trees around it? Is there a swing or any toys lying around? What kind of work are the men and women doing on the house? What are the children up to?

Inside the house, in an upstairs room, the man's wife puts their baby into the crib for a nap. The couple have created a new life, added to their family, out of their love for each other. She looks at the baby, smiles, and pats one of his pink cheeks. Then she goes downstairs.

As the woman passes the playroom, she hears someone crying. A little girl has skinned her knee. The mother comforts her and takes her to clean and bandage the scrape.

As you watch this busy family and see how much they help each other, you realize that God has called you, too, to work with Him as a partner in creation, as a co-creator, to maintain and further the great work of cosmos building. People do little things such as cooking, cleaning, building, and helping others, and they are partners with God in building cosmos. Say a "thank you" to God for creating you in God's own image: as a creative, life-giving person. You are empowered by the breath of God's Spirit, the Ruah, to further the creation process, the cosmos making. Thank God for making you this way, for calling you to create cosmos.

Now picture yourself drawing back from this scene for a star's-eye view of the whole neighborhood, then the county, and the state. From this view, you see that some people have built high walls around their houses so that no one else can get in. Sometimes, walls are built for safety, to keep harm out, but these walls block the view of the slums and the hungry people outside. You see that while some people help others, many people try to exploit their neighbors, cheating them for their own gain. You see that while some people heal, some people harm. You see the dark, destructive chaos that still exists in the people and in the world. This chaos needs to be overcome, to be channeled into creative cosmos-building. What holds you back from the fulfillment, the abundance of life that you will find as God's partner in furthering life, creating cosmos?

From your star's-eye view, see your call to be co-creator with God. See also the way people treat each other. How does God want you to be a builder of cosmos right now? What gifts has God given you? How can you develop and use them now and in the future?

Listen to God tell you how much He wants you to work creatively and compassionately as a partner in building cosmos, in making a better world.

Thank God for calling you to work as a partner in your own way, caring for God's people on earth according to your gifts.

Epilogue:
The Question of Choice

A cartoon depicts a man lying on a couch in the doctor's office. The psychoanalyst explains that life boils down to this: There is a little devil sitting on one shoulder whispering in one ear, while a little angel sits whispering in the other.

Such simple imagery may cause you to laugh, but it address an important dilemma. How much are you responsible for what you do? Is your whole character formed in the playpen? Or by your genes? Does fate dish out your experiences? Or is there room for a choice in what you do? Can you say, "The devil made me do it"?

You are influenced both by your heredity and by others, especially by parents and teachers. Society also plays a role. But for all these factors, you can still make choices.

At the fork in the road of life, which road will you take? The high or the low? The expressway or the back road? Will you take in the scenery along the way, responding to events that unfold? Will you choose action, or will you choose to make no choice at all? Will you choose growth or stagnation, creativity or destruction, life or death, chaos or cosmos?

These grandiose words describe the results of what are usually small decisions. However, your little, everyday choices prepare you for the big moments, the great crossroads you encounter. Making little choices now helps you form habits that will help you handle the big choices later.

One choice is whether to accept or resist opposite personalities you encounter. Accepting them may be difficult, but you open new doors every time you do.

Another choice is whether to live on the surface or to explores the inner dimensions of life, the real "final frontier" beyond even what the starship Enterprise explored.

The crew of the Enterprise often faced death in their heroic adventures, but the basic goals for the characters were integrity and life. In real life, people often ponder the question of whether to live or die. In crisis, this may refer to the death of the physical body. But more often and less obvious, it is a death of the spirit. This occurs, depending on whether you make choices that are life-giving or life-defeating.

By "dying to self," I do not mean overcoming selfishness, unloving attitudes, or bad habits. This choice expands you, in the long run, to promote further life. It goes with the discipline of making inner journeys and winning inner battles. By "choosing death rather than life," I am referring to choices that keep you from reaching your full potential in all dimensions.

This is underscored in Deuteronomy 30:15-20, wherein God invites you to choose life:

> Here, then, I have today set before you life and prosperity, death and doom. If you obey the commandments of the LORD, your God, which I enjoin on you today, loving him, and walking in his ways, and keeping his commandments, statutes and decrees, you will live and grow numerous, and the LORD, your God, will bless you in the land you are entering....I call heaven and earth to witness...I have set before you life and death, the blessing and the curse. Choose life, then, that you and your descendants may live, by loving the LORD, your God, heeding his voice, and holding fast to him (NAB).

You and the whole human race are faced with whether to choose life. The choice presents itself in both small and great ways. When you work for and accomplish a good thing, you choose life.

The emphasis in this book has been on winning the inner battles and taking the inner journey, befriending sources of wisdom deep inside the self. Drawing strength and wisdom from your creative unconscious is part of this, but the reverse is also true. You can form and prepare your unconscious to help you later by instructing it with the conscious choices you make now.

How do you make the choice that is best for you? How do you choose life? Consult Appendix 2 for a checklist of questions worth thinking about.

Appendix 1:
Relaxation Techniques

Meditations are enhanced by relaxed beginnings. Many relaxation techniques are available for getting yourself and others ready for inner journeys.

You may want to use these relaxation techniques before the guided meditations in this book, especially before the healing meditation following chapter three. Even on their own, however, they can ease your tension and bring you to peace.

For active imagination or imagery and healing meditations, sit comfortably. If the situation permits, lie down on the floor. Or, if sleep is your goal, lie on the couch.

RELAXING MUSCLE GROUPS

Take a few deep breaths. Begin to speak to different parts of your body, giving each part directions to relax, relax, relax...

Begin with the feet. Invite them to be at peace, to relax. Travel up through the different muscle groups, one group at a time: legs, knees, thighs, torso (lower and upper, front and back). Continue with the fingertips, hands, upper and lower arms. Work through the shoulders, neck, jaw, and head. Each of these part of the body is invited to "Relax, relax."

The head is especially important. Direct the jaw, forehead, scalp, mouth, nose, and eyes to relax.

FURTHER DIALOGUE WITH YOUR BODY

You can direct your body further by saying to each part, "All you muscles, ligaments, veins, little capillaries and cells, relax; just relax." Think of all the wonderful parts that make up your body; invite them singly, or in small groups, to relax.

The body is intelligent; it wants what is good for it. If you speak to it politely and treat it respectfully, it will comply. However, if you have indulged in too much caffeine, empty calories, food, or drugs that insult the integrity of the body, you may have to eliminate them first before you can achieve true relaxation.

TENSING AND RELAXING

Another approach involves actively tensing each group of muscles, holding them at their tightest for a few seconds, then releasing. Consciously feel the once-tight muscles relax.

Concentration is the key here. Concentrate first on tensing and holding a muscle to the extreme and on how that muscle feels at its tensest. Next concentrate on relaxing to the extreme, saying "Relax, relax, relax." Concentrate on the good feelings that come. Concentrate on each group of muscles, until the entire body is totally relaxed.

IMAGINING A SAFE PLACE

You cannot always do a complete relaxation (at the office, etc.). However, the day may provide times when you most need to tap your inner wisdom and overcome inner obstacles. You can prepare ahead for such times.

After you have finished the above relaxation process, imagine yourself in a beautiful, safe place: a quiet beach or garden or a favorite room. This image becomes an inner resource that enables your spirit to find peace in a few seconds, even when life is hectic. In this inner sanctuary, you can tap inner wisdom even during an emergency. To be effective, however, you must go to this inner place many times after a total relaxation and establish it firmly in your inner world.

The imagery meditations in this book provide more examples of safe, secure places. Choose one that is best for you and stick to it. After some practice on your own during peaceful times, you can go there in your mind even in your most chaotic, everyday moments. There you will find inner peace to help you overcome both internal and external problems.

Appendix 2:
Choices for Life

The following checklist was derived from my own efforts to choose life. It begins with your bodily needs, both sensory and practical. Then it addresses your less-visible needs of the inner self. Feel free to add your own questions.

CHOICES FOR LIFE

Am I making choices for life...

1. ...by avoiding empty calories, by eating moderate amounts of nutritious foods? Do I feed my body with the right amounts of vitamins, minerals, enzymes, etc., that it needs to function well without cravings, fatigue, or poor health? Do I make the effort to prepare good foods in delightful ways, appealing to eye and palate, or do I compliment and support others who do this for me?

2. ...by working my wonderful body, giving it the exercise it needs in a consistent program? Do I offer it times of rest and relaxation, as well as times of satisfying hard work? Do I take care of it as a beautiful, highly effective gift of Life, a vehicle to sustain my journeys and help others on theirs?

3. ...by taking time out to be with nature and art? Do I bring these elements (plants, paintings, music,

good books, etc.) into my life? Do I afford some time and money to nurture my need for beauty? Do I work to make my living space clean, simple, harmonious, peaceful, and enriched with meaningful symbols?

4. ...by firmly choosing, in crisis situations, thoughts that are peacemaking, positive, affirming, and hopeful, so that angry, negative thoughts will not get the upper hand and lead me into further chaos? Do I choose peace rather than conflict so that I am open to inner wisdom and creative solutions to problems?

5. ...by forgiving myself when I make mistakes, seeing what I can learn, and trying again? Do I forgive others when they hurt me or make mistakes, and do I make every effort to be reconciled? Am I ready to be honest with myself and with others so that differences can be resolved and broken relationships can be truly mended?

6. ...by surfacing and confronting hurts, guilts, fears, and pains as they arise and by exploring where they come from? Do I hold my needs up to God for help and healing? Do I enlist the help of a wise, understanding friend or spiritual guide to support and encourage me as I work through these things?

7. ...by making time for inner journeys of meditation and visualization, so that I am open to inner wisdom and the presence of God? Have I developed a mantra (a spiritual formula; a short, memorized prayer) to quiet and calm my mind at difficult times? Do I have a spiritual guide or friends to support me as I go?

8. ...by making time to celebrate with others? Do I develop my gifts and talents that contribute to their

general well-being? Do I make time for family and communal rituals that have meaning? Do I take part in them with my mind and heart?

9. ...by making people a priority? Do I take time to support and affirm family members, friends, co-workers, and others in the community? Am I really present to others? Do I listen to their feelings as well as their thoughts? Do I appreciate others for who they are as well as for what they do? Do I keep close touch with family and community? Am I there for others when they need me?

10. ...by becoming sensitive to God in other people as well as in myself? Am I aware of where there is pain, loneliness, hunger, sickness, or any other need? Do I help, according to my gifts, talents, and resources? Do I actively support the growth of goodness, love, and life with family, friends, community, and world?

Sources and Further Reading

Journey to Life

1. Campbell, Joseph. *The Hero with a Thousand Faces*. New York: Pantheon Books, 1949.

2. Sandars, N. K. *The Epic of Gilgamesh*. English version and introduction. Baltimore: Penguin Books, 1960.

3. "Judith." *The New American Bible*. New York: Thomas Nelson Publishers, 1976.

FURTHER READING

Hazeltine, Alice I. *Hero Tales from Many Lands*. New York and Nashville: Abingdon Press, 1961.

Zipes, Jack, trans. *The Complete Tales of the Brothers Grimm*. New York and Toronto: Bantam Books, 1987.

Journey Past Fear

1. "Tobit." *The New American Bible*. New York: Thomas Nelson Publishers, 1976.

2. Blackie, Margery G. *The Patient, not the Cure: The Challenge of Homoeopathy*. Santa Barbara, CA: Woodbridge Press, 1978.

Clover, Anne. *Homoeopathy, A Patient's Guide*. New York: Thorson's Publishers Inc., 1984.

Cummings, Stephen, and Ullman, Dana. *Homeopathic Medicines*. Los Angeles: Jeremy P. Tarcher Inc., 1984.

3. Numbers 21:4-9. *The New American Bible*. New York: Thomas Nelson Publishers, 1976.

4. Vargiu, James G. "Subpersonalities." *Synthesis* 1, no. 1 (1974). This publication illustrates the active imagination, also known as "waking dream," "guided daydream," or "guided imagery."

5. Williams, Strephon Kaplan. *Jungian-Senoi Dreamwork Manual.* Berkeley: Journal Press, 1980. Page 281. Some questions regarding the Senoi practice of dreams cannot be checked due first to changes in that culture and second to the death of Kilton Stewart. The role of dreams in many other cultures, however, has been more recently verified. Also of import has been the success of people who have worked with some of these principles in the context of their own culture.

6. *Rite of Christian Initiation of Adults, Study Edition.* Collegeville, Minn.: The Liturgical Press, 1988.

Ellebracht, Mary Pierre. *The Easter Passage: The RCIA Experience.* Minneapolis: Winston Press, 1983.

Journey to Healing

1. Sandars, N. K. *The Epic of Gilgamesh.* English version and introduction. Baltimore: Penguin Books, 1960.

2. "The Acts of the Apostles." *The New American Bible.* New York: Thomas Nelson Publishers, 1976.

3. Linn, Dennis and Matthew. *Healing of Memories: Prayer and Confession—Steps to Inner Healing.* Ramsey, New Jersey: Paulist Press, 1974.

_____. *Healing Life's Hurts: Healing Memories Through the Five Stages of Forgiveness.* Mahwah/Ramsey, New Jersey: Paulist Press, 1978.

4. Pelletier, Kenneth R. *Mind As Healer, Mind As Slayer: A Holistic Approach to Preventing Stress Disorders.* New York: Dell Publishing Co., 1977.

5. Siegel, Bernard. *Love, Medicine, and Miracles.* New York: Harper & Row Publishers, Inc., 1986.

6. Selye, Hans. *The Stress of Life.* New York: McGraw-Hill Inc., 1956.

7. Simonton, O. Carl; Stephanie Matthews-Simonton; and James Creighton. *Getting Well Again*. New York: Bantam Books, 1980.

FURTHER READING

Borysenko, Joan. *Minding the Body. Mending the Mind*. Reading, Mass.: Addison-Wesley Publishing Co. Inc., 1987.

Haye, Louise. *You Can Heal Your Life*. Santa Monica, Calif.: Hay House Inc., 1984.

Jaffe, Dennis T. *Healing from Within: Psychological Techniques You Can Use to Help the Mind Heal the Body*. New York: Simon & Schuster Inc., 1980.

Journey Past Crisis

1. Peck, M. Scott. *The Road Less Traveled*. New York: Simon & Schuster Inc., 1978.

2. Schuller, Robert. *The Be-Happy Attitudes*. Waco, Texas: Word Books, 1985.

3. Viorst, Judith. *Necessary Losses*. New York: Simon & Schuster Inc. 1986.

4. "Revelation." *The New American Bible*. New York: Thomas Nelson Publishers, 1976.

Dossey, Larry. *Space, Time, and Medicine*. Boulder, Colorado, and London: Shambhala Publications Inc., 1982.

Prigogine, Ilya, and Isabelle Stengers. *Order out of Chaos: Man's New Dialogue with Nature*. Boulder, Colorado, and London: Shambhala Publications Inc., 1984.

FURTHER READING

Capra, Fritjof. *The Turning Point: Science, Society, and the Rising Culture*. New York: Simon & Schuster Inc., 1984.

Kushner, Harold S. *When Bad Things Happen to Good People*. New York: Avon Books, 1981.

Lauer, Robert H., and Jeannetter C. Lauer. *Watersheds, Mastering Life's Unpredictable Crises*. Boston and Toronto: Little, Brown & Co., 1988.

Journey to Consciousness

1. "Revelation." *The New American Bible.* New York: Thomas Nelson Publishers, 1976.

   D'Aragon, Jean-Louis, SJ. "Apocalypse." *The Jerome Biblical Commentary* no. 23, page 473. Englewood Cliffs, New Jersey: Prentice Hall, 1968.

2. Jung, C. G. *Man and His Symbols.* New York: Doubleday & Co., 1969.

3. Fox, Matthew. *Original Blessing: A Primer in Creation Spirituality.* Santa Fe: Bear & Company, 1983.

4. Hall, Calvin S., and Vernon J. Nordby. *A Primer of Jungian Psychology.* New York: Taplinger Publishing Co. Inc., 1973. This is an excellent book to read, along with Jung's own writings, as a help to gaining an overall picture of the energies, structures, dynamics, relationships, and movements of the human psyche.

   Campbell, Joseph. *Memories, Dreams, and Reflections.* New York: Pantheon Books Inc., 1963.

   _____. *The Undiscovered Self.* Boston: Little, Brown & Co., 1957.

5. Keirsey, David, and Marilyn Bates. *Please Understand Me.* New York: Prometheus/Nemesis, 1978.

Journey to the Unconscious

1. Fromm, Eric. *Escape from Freedom.* New York: Avon Books, 1971.

   All the sources from the previous chapter apply to this chapter with the following additions:

   Goldbrunner, Joseph. *Cure of Mind and Cure of Soul.* Notre Dame: University of Notre Dame Press, 1962.

   Sanford, John. *Invisible Partners.* Mahwah, New Jersey: Paulist Press, 1980.

Journey to Your Higher Self

1. Sanford, John. *Dreams and Healing.* Ramsey, New Jersey: Paulist Press, 1978.

2. Tickle, John. *The Book of Revelation: A Catholic Interpretation of the Bible.* Ligouri, Missouri: Ligouri Publications, 1983.

3. Jung, C. G. *Man and His Symbols.* New York: Doubleday & Co., 1969.

4. Tickle, *Revelation.*

Goldbrunner, Joseph. *Cure of Mind and Cure of Soul.* Notre Dame: University of Notre Dame Press, 1962.

Hall, Calvin S., and Vernon J. Nordby. *A Primer of Jungian Psychology.* New York: Taplinger Publishing Co. Inc., 1973.

Campbell, Joseph, ed. *The Portable Jung.* New York: Viking Penguin Inc., JH - YEAR?

_____. *Memories, Dreams, and Reflections.* New York: Pantheon Books Inc., 1963.

_____. *The Undiscovered Self.* Boston: Little, Brown & Co., 1957.

Sanford, John A. *Dreams: God's Forgotten Language.* Philadelphia and New York: J B Lippincott Co., 1968.

Journey from Chaos to Cosmos

1. "Genesis." *The New American Bible.* New York: Thomas Nelson Publishers, 1976.

2. Hellwig, Monika. *Understanding the Sacraments.* Kansas City: N. C. R. Cassettes, 1975.

3. Fox, Matthew. *Original Blessing.* Santa Fe: Bear & Company, 1978.

4. "Deuteronomy." *The New American Bible.* New York: Thomas Nelson Publishers, 1976.

5. "Revelation." *The New American Bible.* New York: Thomas Nelson Publishers, 1976.

Epilogue: The Question of Choice

1. Jampolsky, Gerald G. *Love Is Letting Go of Fear.* New York: Bantam, 1981.

EXPLORE YOUR SELF IN FIVE NEW WAYS!

CONTEMPLATION AND THE ART OF SALADMAKING

by Jeanne Heiberg
Paperbound $8.95, 234 pages, 5 ½" X 8 ½"
ISBN 0-8245-0435-6

If you can achieve a tasteful combination of ingredients in the salad bowl, then you can achieve the right blend of physical, emotional, and spiritual ingredients in your life. By the author of ***Winning Your Inner Battle***.

"A delightful little cookbook...This book is fun...The author presents easy-reading anecdotes about friends and others, usually leading to her own philosophies and to some easy, delectable recipes." — Audrey Allen, columnist, *The Tablet*

"I challenge you to find a better collection of stories, tips on nutrition, recipes, and spiritual counsel between two covers of any one book." — Doris Donnelly, Princeton Theological Seminary, author of *Learning to Forgive.*

WHISPERS OF THE HEART: A Journey Toward Befriending Yourself

by Dale R. Olen
Paperbound, $8.95, 180 pages, 5 ½" X 8 ½"
ISBN 0-89390-100-8

Behavior arises from fundamental core energies that are good: the energy to exist, the energy to act freely, the energy to love. Get in touch with these energies and learn to celebrate your own goodness. Your behavior will improve, as well as your sense of fulfillment and growth.

THE DEBRIS OF THE ENCOUNTER: A Recovery of Self

by Terre Ouwehand
Paperbound $7.95, 75 pages, 5 ½" X 8 ½"
ISBN 0-89390-137-7

Whether you're searching for the Spirit or trying to renew or strengthen your faith, ***The Debris of the Encounter*** will take you there. A book of sensual poetry and vivid prose, the works are "spiritual souvenirs" of the author's experiences. On a spiritual level, you'll find new channels to explore and strengthen you; on a literary level, you'll appreciate these carefully crafted works of art.

BIBLICAL BLUES
Growing Through Set-Ups and Let-Downs
by Andre Papineau
Paperbound, $7.95, 160 pages, 5 ½" x 8 ½"
ISBN 0-89390-157-1, November 1989
This book of biblical stories will take you deep into your own personal recovery and transform you. The author, whose dramatic tales always have a psychological edge, here addresses the way people set themselves up for a let-down. Jesus, ever the playful one, often enters the scene to puncture a balloon, a deflating event that can lead to spiritual growth.

DISCOVERING MY BIBLICAL DREAM HERITAGE
by Lois Lindsey Hendricks
Paperbound $9.95, 250 pages, 5 ½" X 8 ½"
ISBN 0-89390-144-X
What do your dreams mean to you as a Christian? In this refreshing approach to Bible study, the author shows you the function of dreams in biblical stories. In non-technical language, she details the dreamers and dreams found in the Hebrew Bible, the Apocrypha, and the New Testament. She then relates them to her own dreams, at the same time guiding you to find the spiritual meaning in yours.

"Lois Hendricks reminds us of our deep cultural roots in dreaming. Well done!" — Jayne Gackenback, Ph.D., president of the Association for the Study of Dreams

"Lois shows us how the study of dreams in the Bible and in one's nightly life can enrich both our appreciation for the religious and the daily problem solving functions of dreaming." — Gayle M. V. Delaney, Ph.D., founding president of the Association for the Study of Dreams

"Hendricks shows us that God's presence in our lives through dreams has not ceased..." — Louis M. Savary, co-author of *Dreams and Spiritual Growth*

ORDER FORM

Order from your local religious bookstore, or mail this form to: **Resource Publications, Inc.**
160 E. Virginia St., Suite 290
San Jose, CA 95112
(408) 286-8505

Qty	Title	Price	Total
____	_____	____	____
____	_____	____	____
____	_____	____	____
____	_____	____	____
____	_____	____	____

Subtotal _____

California residents add 6% sales tax _____

*Postage & Handling _____

Total amount enclosed _____

*Postage & Handling
$1.50 for orders under $10.00
$2.00 for orders of $10.00-$25.00
9% (max. $7.00) of order for orders over $25.00

☐ My check or money order is enclosed.

☐ Charge my ☐Visa ☐MC   Exp. date: _____

Card No. ____-____-____-____

Signature: _____

Name: _____

Institution: _____

Street: _____

City: _____ State ____ Zip ____

Code:WI